for laura and sharon

maggie and milly and molly and may
went down to the beach(to play one day)

and maggie discovered a shell that sang
so sweetly she couldn't remember her troubles,and

milly befriended a stranded star
whose rays five languid fingers were;

and molly was chased by a horrible thing
which raced sideways while blowing bubbles:and

may came home with a smooth round stone
as small as a world and as large as alone.

For whatever we lose(like a you or a me)
it's always ourselves we find in the sea

e.e. cummings

DWELLERS IN THE SEA

Photographs and Commentary
by DOUGLAS FAULKNER

Text by BARRY FELL

READER'S DIGEST PRESS

Distributed by Thomas Y. Crowell Company

New York
1976

"maggie and milly and molly and may" Copyright, 1956, by E.E. Cummings. "o sweet spontaneous" Copyright, 1923, 1951, by E.E. Cummings. Both reprinted from his volume, *Complete Poems 1913-1962,* by permission of Harcourt Brace Jovanovich, Inc., New York.

"Pied Beauty" is from *Poems of Gerard Manley Hopkins,* Fourth Edition, edited by W.H. Gardiner and N.H. MacKenzie, published by Oxford University Press, New York.

LIBRARY OF CONGRESS CATALOGING IN PUBLICATION DATA
Faulkner, Douglas.
    Dwellers in the sea.

    Bibliography: p.
    1. Marine fauna.   I. Fell, Barry.   II. Title.
QL121.F25   591.9'2   76-17286

ORIGINATED AND PRODUCED BY VISUAL BOOKS, INC., 342 MADISON AVENUE, NEW YORK, NEW YORK 10017.

CONTENTS

ILLUSTRATIONS

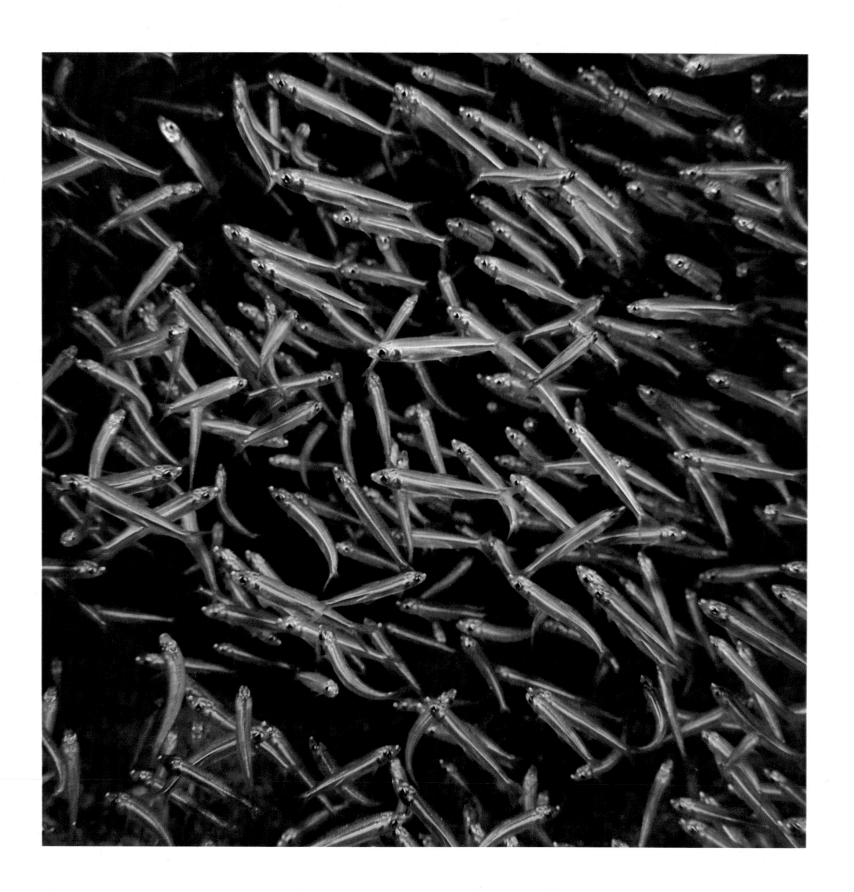

DWELLERS IN THE SEA

AEGEAN PRELUDE

Three thousand years ago a bold Aegean mariner plunged from his ship to the seabed and contrived to surface unharmed, initiating that peculiarly Greek athletic skill, free diving.

Later, as centuries went by, Mediterranean travelers carried the art to the Egyptian shores, to Libya, to the Red Sea coasts, and on to the Indies and the far Pacific, where Polynesians practiced it before the time of Bougainville and Cook. In the Old World it remained a skill particularly associated with the Aegean peoples, most of them Greeks, and it is in Greek literature that we find the earliest references to *dytēs*—the divers. When the Trojan charioteer Kebriones falls headlong to the earth, slain by Patroklos, the Greek exclaims sarcastically: "Why, see now, the Trojans have divers among them—now if only this man were at sea, how nimbly he might have plunged overboard to gather seafood!" Homer wrote it; a Greek viewpoint in 800 B.C.

Diving seems to have been unknown in Egypt until relatively late in her history, though Egyptian sailors were expert in the use of trawls and nets for harvesting the deep. When diving did reach that country, toward Coptic times, it was used especially by pearl fishers.

Until modern times free diving remained the prerogative of maritime peoples of the warmer seas, seeking a livelihood by hard-won hauls of sponges, corals, pearl shell, and occasionally pearls. The working diver's lifespan was short. The physical and physiological strain inherent in his occupation was intense.

Then, in a secluded bay on the French coast during World War II a detachment of naval officers under the leadership of Jacques-Yves Cousteau, strengthened by the engineering skill of Émile Gagnon, gave to the world the aqualung, and man became free to roam the oceans at will. In the years since then probably a million people have experienced the wonder of visiting the underwater environment. Aided by cameras of superb quality, diver-biologists can now permit all of us, in the comfort of our homes, to share their fascinating experiences. When science is combined with artistry, the result is pictures such as those of Douglas Faulkner; images that delight the eye but also make one think about man's long journey from the seashore to the world beneath the waves.

That journey began some ten thousand years ago, appropriately in France. There, on some vanished foreshore of the Bay of Biscay, long ago swallowed up by the rising sea level as the polar ice caps melted, a nameless tribe of Stone Age people gained a livelihood from the sea. Men had done the same, no doubt, for thousands of years before that, but these people —perhaps remote ancestors of the Basques—introduced something new. They not only gathered shellfish for food but acquired a perception of beauty. For the first time, so far as we can tell, these waifs of the receding ice collected the shells of the mollusks they ate and strung them together to make the world's first jewelry. Nor was that all. Exercising another human propensity, they traded their wares with inland tribes, and one item, a necklace of shells sorted symmetrically by size and shape, found its way to a cave in the Dordogne district. This Cro-Magnon dwelling was excavated about a century ago, to yield material evidence of ancient commerce based upon the harvest of the seas.

The fascinating and mysterious seashells soon became the accepted standard of wealth among the shore people and the inland tribes. Currency may be said to have begun at this time. With it came that other facet of human behavior, deception. Wandering prospectors discovered that somewhat similar objects could be obtained inland, in the shape of fossil seashells, bleached and stained, but nonetheless recognizable simulacra of the colored objects cast up by the ocean. From ancient sites once inhabited by man all over Europe we find necklaces and pendants of fossil shells, which soon became the jewels of the common people. Now, with this lowering of the currency value, only the most highly polished, colorful, and porcelanous shells could be reckoned as "sterling." The gleaming and tinted cowries of the warmer coasts had no rival as convenient units for the measure and exchange of wealth, and they could not be found as fossils. International currency had arrived, and there are still parts of the world, far from the sea, where cowrie currency is to be reckoned officially as a submetallic coinage, and where a bride-price may be reckoned in strings of shell. So from the sea came man's first international coinage.

Twenty centuries pass as the Biscayne shore dwellers and others like them elsewhere in Europe gaze wonderingly upon the restless waters, or scan the distant horizon to glimpse sometimes, on a clear day, the mysterious shadowy image of some far-off coast, or the hills of an unknown land that seems to float upon the ocean itself. What lands are these that beckon so enticingly?

Perhaps about 8000 B.C. some unrecorded watcher from Cape Malea in Greece devised the means of crossing the narrow seas that separate Sparta from the island of Crete. For it is on that island that we find the clearest indications that Neolithic man learned to make boats and to sail them to distant landings. Amber beads, that can have come only from northern Europe, rest among the archaeological relics of the earliest human settlements not far from the place where mighty Knossos was later to rise and flourish. Thus men became mariners and learned to challenge the sea itself. Divine aid was needed in so daring a venture, and the oldest paintings of ships often show an image of the mother goddess carried amidships, seemingly as protectress. Later the sea itself was deified and seen as a male divinity, perhaps thereby more amenable to the wiles of the mother goddess. In Greece they called his name Poseidon, but whatever name he carried in other lands, his sex was never in doubt. The sea, mighty, tempestuous or calm, became the new highroad of the adventurer.

Crete, famed homeland of sea kings, forms the western extremity of the world's most enchanting archipelago, the Aegean realm, where unnumbered islands spawned a race of hardy sailors. Of all the islands there, Crete alone proved large enough to engender and maintain a stable civil administration. In Crete, during the second millennium before Christ, there arose a self-contained civilization, called by modern archaeologists Minoan, in reference to one of its mythical kings. Beginning as a home-based rural economy, Crete extended her maritime contacts until, by about 1500 B.C., she could send fleets of wind-powered ships across the Mediterranean to Egypt, to

trade with pharaohs of the eighteenth dynasty. Egyptian painters recorded these embassies on stone, and their deft delineation of costume and trade wares has given us a vivid picture of what the hieroglyphs call "the Princes of the Isles that lie in the Great Green Sea." The excavations of Sir Arthur Evans in Crete brought to light the palaces and temples of these princes, whose wall paintings and artifacts speak of a people devoted to the ways of the sea.

About 1250 B.C. Crete came under a new administration, when invading Myceneans from the north occupied the land and introduced the Greek language. But her maritime traditions lived on to become a heritage of the Greeks. A mysterious age of barbarism intervened after 1000 B.C., but when Greek writers such as Hesiod and Homer renewed the mainspring of literature about 800 B.C., the maritime tradition was still overwhelming. All our oldest Greek heroes are men who sailed to Troy and other foreign parts, or even passed through the Gates of Hercules to visit the Atlantic coast of Spain, as Agamemnon is said to have done. Most of the *Odyssey* and a part of the *Iliad* are devoted to ships and sailing, and even Hesiod, though he sings to farmers, does not omit giving detailed hints on seafaring and the maintenance of ships in summer and winter. As the art of Greece changes in response to the flowering of the classical Greek civilization, it, too, reflects marine themes, and then, finally, with the rise of Greek science, Aristotle presents us with a textbook on animal life, much of which is given over to marine biology, based in part on his own researches at his two marine biological research stations, the one in Mytilene, the other in Euboea.

Aristotle taught the principle that inference should be based upon observation, and his remarks on marine animals are commonly supported by information he obtained by dissecting them or by watching their behavior in the sea. He counted Greek sailors among his informants and companions, and it is with this remarkable Greek philosopher, the tutor of Alexander the Great, that we of the modern world can most easily empathize. He saw the works of Nature as the orderly outcome of definable influences, and therein lies his accessibility to twentieth-century man. When he made mistakes, as he often did, they are mistakes of a kind that we, too, or our more immediate predecessors, might make. Medieval mysticism had no part in Aristotle's world, and we can therefore communicate more easily with Greeks of twenty-three centuries past than we can with our own superstitious forebears of Europe's Middle Ages.

In reality Greek thought never wholly died in the West, and there were monks who carefully preserved the Hellenic tradition in the libraries of the monasteries of Italy, France, and England, for there can be no doubt that modern science stems from that of Greece.

ARGOSIES
IN CORAL SEAS

Corals and sea anemones are among the most beautiful and interesting of all sea dwellers. Greek authors do not have much to say on the subject, probably because there are no coral reefs in the Mediterranean, and it was not until Greek captains began to sail the Red Sea and the Indian Ocean that these remarkable features of tropical waters came to their attention.

The poet Pindar wrote in the fifth century B.C. of a wreath of honor that had been carved from ivory, gold, and "the lily of the sea." Some have supposed that he referred to coral. The word used in Greek, *koralleion,* is the origin of our own modern term for coral, but scholars think it is not really a Greek word and that it may have been borrowed from one of the languages spoken along the Red Sea coasts in ancient times. As for the sea anemones, these were called actinia by the Greeks.

Sea anemones, common in rock pools, are a well-known feature of seashore life. The gelatinous body of an anemone is shaped like a cylinder, with a mouth opening at the upper end, surrounded by rings of stinging adhesive tentacles by which small organisms are captured as food. Anemones are often brightly colored, almost resembling flowers, but even to the ancients their movements betrayed their animal nature. Corals are essentially sea anemones that have acquired a skeleton, either a stony lime cup, in which

the animal is seated, or a hornlike material, as in the corals called alcyonarians. Corals may be solitary animals, with a single mouth opening surrounded by a wreath of tentacles, as is the case in anemones, or they may be colonial, in which a large number of miniaturized anemone-like individuals are all in organic connection, sharing a common skeleton. These were more puzzling to the ancients, who usually thought of them as sea trees, with branches, the individual coral animals being regarded as the flowers.

When Alexander conquered India and the rest of the Old World, he is said to have remembered his old tutor, and to have ordered that specimens of the fauna and flora of foreign lands, or details about them, were to be sent home to Greece for the use of Aristotle. But, somehow, corals were overlooked, for Aristotle has nothing to say about them in his surviving books. We learn from Latin authors that Indian buyers set a high price upon the precious red coral of Italy and Sicily and readily traded their own pearls for it, an exchange very much to the Romans' liking.

The Roman naturalist-economist, Pliny the Elder, has much to report on the Indian trade of the first century A.D. Pliny explains that Indian buyers were anxious to obtain Roman coral because their priests credited the red substance with the power of warding off the Evil Eye. He mentions, too, that the Gauls in France had a similar veneration for red coral and used it to adorn their swords and shields. The voyage to India and back to Suez again required three years, for mariners feared to go beyond the sight of land and were obliged to follow the tortuous Asian coast, putting ashore each night and paying imposts to the Arab chieftains along the route.

One of the great discoveries of oceanography was made by a Greek captain, Hippalos, about 30 A.D. Greek captains who commanded the merchant ships of Alexandria were aware that a prevailing monsoon wind blew from the southwest, across the Arabian Sea, each summer, bringing heavy rain to India from the moisture picked up during the passage of the wind across the sea; also that a wind in the opposite direction came from northeast India in winter. Hippalos, using the southwest monsoon, abandoned the coastal route and crossed the Arabian Sea directly from Aden to India, completing the voyage in three months. He capped his triumph by returning by the same route, using the northeast monsoon. Within twelve months—instead of the usual three years—he completed a round-trip voyage from Egypt to India and back.

The pioneering of Hippalos led eventually to the discovery that great wind belts exist on the surface of the earth, blowing with remarkable regularity over particular tracts of the oceans. It was one of these, the trade wind of the tropical Atlantic, that carried Columbus to America, and another of them, the west-wind-belt or anti-trade, that brought Columbus back to Europe by way of the northern part of the North Atlantic. Ancient inscriptions found in America and the Canary Islands confirm that these Atlantic winds were already known to sailors of Libya and Spain long before the time of Christ, but the pioneering of Hippalos in the Indian Ocean stands as the first formal record.

For the scuba diver the story of the sea winds is pertinent, for all the major currents of the oceans flow in the same direction as the prevailing winds in each latitude. A convincing proof of this is given by the Somali Current, that flows to the east of Arabia and northeast Africa. Here, as Hippalos discovered, the oceanic wind blows from the northeast for half of the year, and then reverses to blow from the southwest for the other half of the year. Each time the wind reverses its direction, the Somali Current also reverses.

When Hadrian became emperor of Rome, Greek and Graeco-Egyptian shipping began to cross the great Bay of Bengal to Burma, thereafter sailing into Indonesia, traversing the narrow waters between Sumatra (Ophir) and Malaya, to pass through the Straits of Malacca and enter the North Pacific. These early voyages seem to have been forgotten by most historians in the West, who assign a greatly exaggerated importance to European navigators of the fifteenth century.

It is plain from the Chinese records that Greek and Roman vessels were now navigating waters that carry the richest coral reef faunas in the world.

What were the ships that made these protracted expeditions? Doubtless they were wind-powered single-masted vessels, carrying oars for use in emergencies when the wind failed, but not otherwise oar-propelled, for a large crew would eliminate any prospect of making a profit. Much of the financing of such long voyages must have been carried out by the banking houses of Rome, whose shareholders would certainly expect the return cargoes to include pearls, highly valued by the Roman matrons.

It, therefore, seems probable that the crews of these vessels carried experts in the Greek art of free diving, and that underwater vistas on tropical Pacific reefs were already being glimpsed by men from the Mediterranean ports, twelve centuries before medieval Europe gained an awareness of the Orient.

SPONGES AND JELLYFISHES

Sponges are the most simply organized of all marine animals. In our modern age of plastics the word "sponge" is commonly applied to synthetic materials, such as foam rubber, filled with countless small bubbles of air. They have elasticity combined with the power of absorbing temporarily a large amount of water, which can be easily expelled from the sponge material by squeezing it. But the original use of the word was for the dried body of a marine organism that had the same spongy character, the organism that the Greeks called "spongos," and it is from the Greeks that we acquired our word.

Sponges look like brightly tinted plants, vaguely recalling fungi. Their true nature baffled the ancients, for in some ways they seemed to be real plants, in others more like animals. For example, if a predatory animal browses on a sponge, biting off pieces just as if they were so much herbage, the amputated residual stump soon grows again, to restore the creature to its former appearance and size. Or if a tempest disturbs the sea floor and tears a sponge in half, each of the severed portions can grow into an entire sponge. Yet again, if two sponges grow toward each other and come into direct contact, they will, if they belong to the same species, fuse to make a single large sponge. Most of the ancient writers thought of sponges as some kind of marine weed. But there are a few sponges whose body tissues include muscular fibers that will contract slowly if touched or irritated. Apparently Aristotle noticed this, for he correctly inferred, about 350 B.C., that sponges are animals.

Paddle a boat over a shallow reef where large sponges can be seen on the sunlit sea floor beneath. If you watch the surface of the lagoon water carefully, you may soon discover that a kind of volcanic eruption seems to be taking place—for a strong, ascending current of water is reaching the surface, directly over each of the larger sponges. On a much smaller scale a similar observation was made under a microscope 150 years ago by a Scottish naturalist called Grant, who was one of Darwin's teachers. It is in fact the clue to how a sponge lives and why it is really an animal. For the current of water is emitted from the osculum—a large central opening leading to the central cavity of the sponge—and consists of filtered seawater from which the sponge has extracted all digestible floating bacteria. The sponge obtains this finely divided food material by sucking in water through its numerous pores, filtering the water through internal chambers where the bacteria are digested, and then expelling the filtered water as a single stream from the osculum. Plants utilize dissolved minerals, not solid bacteria, as food, and this is the critical difference that classifies sponges as animals. They are an ancient type of animal life, for their fossilized remains, at least 600 million years old, can be found in the hardened sea floor sediments of ancient oceans.

Sponges are depicted in wall paintings of Crete from about 1700 B.C. In one they are shown growing on a sea floor above which a school of flying fish sports. This charming scene decorates an ancient building at Phylakopi. For written references to sponges the oldest source seems to be Homer, some nine hundred years after the Cretan fresco was painted. Homer tells why the Greek divers collected sponges: as a means of filtering wine and for washing down refectory tables! Later sources state that early painters in watercolor and in wax used dried sponges for applying the color. It was left for Aristotle to discuss the nature of the sponge, in his *Natural History of Animals*. Virtually no advance in understanding sponges was made through the intervening centuries until the time of Grant. So truly the Greeks are the direct predecessors of modern naturalists in this regard.

One of the distinctive features of our planet is the blue of the sea. Photographs taken of earth from outer space always show it as a blue sphere, dappled by much white cloud and the less evident terra-cotta or greenish shapes of the land masses. These colors are produced in part by the atmosphere, whose gases absorb the red part of the sun's spectrum, leaving the blue part to reach the earth's surface, so that when we look up the sky appears blue; and in part also by the property of seawater, which absorbs red light in much the same way. Thus the deeper you dive, the bluer the water becomes, though the total amount of light also diminishes, making the blue of deep water seem very near to black. In early photographs of the seabed the blue light overwhelmed all other colors, so filters and lights were used to compensate for this effect.

The heavenly blue that overlies and envelops the scuba diver when the water is free from sediment and when the tropical sunlight is reaching the wave surface unimpeded by cloud or fog becomes a perfect background against which to see drifting herds of plankton. These organisms exist in countless billions in the surface layers and midwaters of the oceans, but most of them are so minute as to escape the diver's eye. Only the larger, more spectacular plankton organisms can be detected by the naked eye, and most of these are animals. The most conspicuous of them are the jellyfishes, or Scyphozoa as naturalists call them. They seem, to a diver on the sea floor gazing upward, like birds to a sky gazer on land, though their motion is much slower and they float rather than fly.

Perhaps your first or only acquaintance with jellyfishes has been with bedraggled and pathetic chunks of glassy or gelatinous material washed up by the tide, to wither and die in the desiccating breeze of some coast you have visited. You might well wonder what manner of creature is represented by such inert and amorphous shapes, but from underwater things look very different.

There can be no doubt that the gelatinous creatures are indeed animals. They are actively swimming by convulsive contractions and expansions of a circular disk from which descend in graceful swathes a variable number of trailing appendages, the tentacles by which the jellyfish captures its prey. In the center, below the circular swimming bell so like a parachute, lies the mouth, bordered by four trailing fleshy lobes. The trailing tentacles are provided with knots of stinging cells with which the animal touches and then stings and paralyzes its prey. The mouth leads into a capacious digestive chamber or stomach from which the undigestible fragments of victims are from time to time ejected through the mouth, for these strange animals have no intestine and therefore no anal opening.

In the chilling waters of the far northern seas some jellyfish reach a diameter of 2 meters, and their total bulk may amount to one ton. Yet these are not the most dangerous, for there are venomous species of much lesser dimension, armed with stinging cells that can paralyze a man. Most kinds are less dangerous, and may do no more than inflict a burning sting that passes off in a while. *Urtica marina,* or "sea nettle," was a name the Romans used for these animals.

The floating and drifting organisms of the sea are collectively called plankton, a term coined a century ago by the German biologist Haeckel from a Greek word that means to drift or float. Animals that live on the floor of the sea, such as sea stars or oysters, are collectively called benthos, from another Greek root meaning deep dwellers. The ancient naturalists knew, of course, about jellyfishes, and they also knew about the ancient Greek actinia, those flowerlike animals that we call sea anemones. But one thing they did not know is that the eggs of jellyfishes first grow into a minute kind of sea anemone, or polyp as it is called, attached to the floor of the sea like a true sea anemone. Later this polyp stage forms tiny buds, each of which is a miniature jellyfish that eventually breaks off and swims away. This complicated life history is one of the pieces of evidence that links jellyfishes and sea anemones as related groups of animals. They are therefore classified together in the same major grouping, to which corals are also assigned.

Think what this means in the ecology of the sea. If you are a diver, you will have seen the plankton animals slowly drifting past you, borne by the current of the particular part of the sea in which you have chosen to immerse yourself. In contrast, the benthos at your feet has scarcely changed: some of the more mobile

bottom dwellers, such as the sea stars, may have moved just a little, though in random directions in no way related to the current; others such as the oysters are permanently cemented to the bottom. The sea anemones have remained attached, while their distant relatives, the jellyfishes, have slowly drifted past.

In time the plankton will be several kilometers away, traveling with the current, and after some months they will have traversed several thousand kilometers. In fact they may have crossed an ocean and be drifting past the coastline of another continent. But all this time the benthos has remained where it was. An ocean current usually travels at a rate of at least 5 kilometers a day, often as much as 12 kilometers a day, and sometimes even 25 kilometers in a single day. The direction of flow is usually such as to form great circular sweeps, the water crossing and recrossing the ocean like a slowly rotating whirlpool.

Floating and swimming animals partake in the motion of the current, and fishes that have had identification tags fixed to them in places like Florida and Cape Cod in New England may turn up in the nets of fishermen off Norway some months later, having drifted across the Atlantic in the Gulf Stream that flows north from Florida, and in the North Atlantic drift that flows eastward from Cape Cod. Similarly fishes that have been tagged on European coasts will later turn up on the North American coast, having made the passage from east to west on the equatorial current that strikes west from the Canary Islands and leads into the Caribbean.

Floating animals like jellyfishes are too soft for identification tags, but doubtless they share the same transoceanic adventures as fishes. Some fishes cannot survive a change of temperature, and when the current begins to sweep them northward from the Gulf area into the cooler waters of New England, they swim southward to recover their original warm habitat. Because fishes, with their strong swimming fins, can do this, ecologists refer to them as nekton, or swimmers, and they are not subject to the inexorable drift that affects plankton. But many fishes are too small to be able to counteract the current; these, if they are vulnerable to changes in temperature, are doomed to die. Every summer millions of little tropical fishes drift northward past Cape Cod, eventually to meet this fate somewhere in the cold mid-Atlantic. On the other hand, powerful swimmers, such as tuna fish, though quite able to swim in the reverse direction to the current, do not in fact do so, for they are not affected adversely by changes in temperature. Of the jellyfishes, most of the species that live in the waters of Europe are found also in the mid-Atlantic and off the coasts of New England and the other North American Atlantic states. These certainly are experienced travelers, crossing and recrossing the Atlantic. Thus sea animals are subject to different influences according to their manner of life, and related members of the same natural group may have very different fates if their habits of life place them in different ecological niches.

There are other effects of ocean currents that a scuba diver is not likely to observe, for the organisms concerned are too tiny to be seen with the unaided eye. For example, many animals of the benthos live a quite opposite life-style to that of the jellyfish. Whereas the jellyfish is planktonic in the adult state, but benthic in the young polyp phase, there are other creatures such as sea urchins that are benthic in the adult state but planktonic in the young phase. The eggs of sea urchins, for example, hatch out into tiny floating larvae that temporarily form a part of the plankton, until they metamorphose into the adult and then sink to the bottom.

One of the major problems of oceanographic research this past decade has been to determine whether benthic animals of Europe and North America can cross the Atlantic while in their juvenile planktonic stages. Results so far have shown that larval stages of European and west African and east American benthos do indeed occur in the open ocean as floating plankton. Whether they live long enough to make a complete passage from one side to the other is still very much an open question, but it seems likely that some species can do this, and if this is true it will help to explain why we find some benthic species living on both sides of the Atlantic.

There are more ways than one to cross an ocean. Drifting logs far out to sea can carry a miniature population of barnacles and mollusks and even an occasional sea urchin, clinging to the lower side immersed in the sea. Such a Noah's ark may occasionally make a complete journey across an ocean, to deliver its living cargo on the opposite shore. Sometimes great tangles of floating kelp have coastal benthic animals on board. Rafts of this kind, sometimes with logs interlocked, can reach a length of 15 meters, and may well be capable of crossing an ocean.

Benthic animals cannot simply creep across the bottom of the Atlantic, which is four kilometers deep, for shallow-water benthos is never found alive at such immense depths. On the other hand, benthos could, conceivably, slowly spread around the northern polar margin of the Atlantic, where the seabed is much shallower, though this would require a tolerance for low temperatures.

In all the conjecture, one thing is certain—many of the marine organisms that a scuba diver in Europe observes are identical, or nearly identical, with corresponding species on the American shoreline.

REEF CORALS

Corals are marine animals. There are several kinds of corals, differing according to the internal symmetry of the organs in the body, and also differing in the number of tentacles that form the petals around the mouth of each coral animal. These differences can be seen quite clearly, and have been recorded with close-up photography.

By far the greatest number of corals have their internal organs, and tentacles, arranged in multiples of six. These are called hexacorals. Another characteristic that makes them easy to recognize is the hard consistency of the skeleton they form. The skeleton bleaches to a white or grayish color in dead coral. Curio dealers in tropical countries tint coral with artificial dyes, giving the specimens a very unnatural appearance.

Many other groups of corals are brilliantly tinted by nature, and retain much of their color after death. These include the octocorals, with an eight-part symmetry, and with a single ring of eight tentacles around the mouth of each coral. The tentacles are usually branched like a fern frond. The secreted skeleton in octocorals is a mixture of hard spicules embedded in a hornlike cement called keratin. The skeleton is most often tinted red or orange. The peculiar organ-pipe coral, *Tubipora,* is found in the Indian and Pacific Oceans; also the corals called sea fans and sea whips. A small group of corals called hydrocorals also form purple or red skeletons; these when alive can inflict a painful sting. Yet another type, black coral, is found in deeper water, not forming part of a reef. When taken from the water, black coral resembles dead tree branches.

A reef is any elevated portion of the seabed so shallow that it approaches the sea surface. A coral reef is composed of pure coral or of rock capped by coral. A living coral reef has actively growing corals on its surface, the remainder of its mass made up of the accumulated skeletons of former living members. Reef corals can grow down to a depth of 50 meters. Below that depth the water is generally too cold and the sunlight too feeble for them.

Coral reefs are confined to tropical and subtropical seas, lying within 30° of latitude north and south of the equator, for reef-building corals cannot live successfully in water of a temperature below 16° C. They occupy a belt that covers half the earth's surface, and they form a well-defined geographic region. If the oceans evaporated, a broad band of coral would be seen, girdling the planet at the equator.

There are three different types of coral reefs. The fringing reef forms near the shoreline on a seabed that slopes steeply. The barrier reef forms far from the shoreline—up to a hundred kilometers or more—on a seabed that slopes very gradually. A broad shallow lagoon region separates it from the coastline. An atoll, or ring-shaped reef, was formed originally as a fringing reef around an islet. When the islet sank, only the atoll reef was left. Atolls of this type occur mainly in the tropical Pacific, where the seabed has been sinking gradually for millions of years.

A living coral reef is a complicated community made up not only of various kinds of corals but also of many associated plants and animals. The chief plants are the microscopic one-celled algae called Diatoms, not visible to the naked eye, but present in large numbers, and the various red algae of the type called corallines, which also secrete limy material, like the coral animals. The animals include numerous mollusks, often brilliantly colored, sea stars and sea urchins, crabs and other crustaceans, and numerous fishes. On the reef itself the fauna and flora are either attached to the bottom or free roaming on the bottom. In the lagoon area, where the bottom is silt or sand, much of the fauna is imbedded in the bottom material and not visible unless disturbed. The swimming animals, principally the fishes, swim or hover over the bottom. The presence of such a variety of organisms, coupled with the circulating oceanic input of dissolved salts, means that the coral reef community is a self-contained ecosystem, the plants providing the organic synthetic foods, the herbivores grazing upon these, the carnivores preying upon the grazing animals, and bacteria recycling the dead material and returning dissolved minerals for use by the plants. The productivity of a coral reef might be increased if more seawater could be cycled through the reef, and there are proposals to do this by artificial means, as a way of increasing the production of edible fish.

Corals, mollusks, and some other animals that secrete large amounts of lime do so in regular daily cycles of activity controlled by the varying availability of food according to the time of day. Reef corals, for example, feed at night and are inactive in daylight hours. This causes the layers of lime in the skeleton to be laid down in regular increments, called growth lines. If the growth lines are readily visible, as they are in some species, then the age of a specimen can be measured by counting the lines.

The growth lines of a coral are thicker in summer than they are in winter when the water temperatures are lower and the daily activity is less. On reefs that lie on the equator the water temperature does not vary much during the year, but in reefs that lie near the northern or southern margins of the tropics there is considerable variation, and these differences show up in the growth lines of the corals, where annual cycles of growth can be recognized in the skeleton. It is possible to determine from such corals that the year's growth is made up of a set of approximately 360 daily growth

had begun an inquiry into Newton's theory that the tides of the ocean are raised by the gravitational attraction of the moon. There had seemed to be a flaw in Newton's argument, because it would seem to imply that high tide ought to occur when the moon passes overhead, yet the records kept at various ports showed very definitely that there is a delay of several hours after the moon crosses the meridian before high tide takes place.

Laplace, after comparing the degree of delay at various ports in Africa and America, observed first that the delay is much more on the American side of the Atlantic than on the African side. He then went on to discover the laws that relate the delay to the depth of the water over which the tide is raised, and the rate at which the tidal wave crosses an ocean of any given depth. He found that to make it possible for the high tide to take place at the moment when the moon is passing over the meridian, the sea would have to be some 20 kilometers deep. For the tide to suffer the observed delays of up to seven hours on the American side of the Atlantic, he found that the Atlantic Ocean must have an actual average depth of about 4 kilometers. This became his calculated estimate of the average depth of the Atlantic Ocean. One century later British oceanographers obtained the first experimental evidence of the depth of the world's oceans, and it became apparent that Laplace was correct. Although the ocean floor drops in a few places to much greater depths, the average depth is indeed 4 kilometers, and this figure applies to all the world oceans.

Another area of debate was whether marine life could survive in deep water. In the early nineteenth century the great Scottish naturalist Edward Forbes declared that below a depth of 300 fathoms (one third of a mile) no life can exist. He had dredged the floor of the Mediterranean, and his results led him to this conclusion, which seemed consistent with the evident lack of light at great depths and the consequential lack of plants to generate carbohydrates. So matters continued until the year 1864, when the scientific world was rudely awakened to the fact that Forbes's conclusions were entirely false.

Forbes had been misled by the fact that his rather crude sampling devices simply did not function at great depths. They returned to the surface empty because they were not sufficiently well designed to catch and retain possession of bottom-dwelling animals when his line exceeded some 300 fathoms in length. Two Norwegians now entered the picture.

East of Lofoten Fjord, within the Arctic Circle, the floor of the ocean drops rather steeply to a depth of 1700 fathoms, or nearly two miles. Upon these cold, mysterious waters just over a century ago, the pioneering techniques of deep-water sampling were first developed by Georg Ossian Sars.

Sars studied the techniques of the local fishermen and then adapted and improved them until he acquired the skill to make bottom collections in offshore deep water. One day in 1864 his line brought up something unusual—a tiny yellow crinoid, an animal quite closely related to shallow water feather stars, though belonging to a different group. Like the feather stars it had feathery branched arms, but unlike them it also had an anchoring stem ending in a tuft of threads that were evidently a kind of rooting to hold it in the soft seabed. It was a living sea lily, an echinoderm related to the feather stars that occur on tropical reefs. But whereas feather stars have a temporary larval stage in which they are anchored to the seabed by a stem, this animal, like fossils that were already known, retained the stem in the adult stage.

The discovery of *Rhizocrinus lofotensis* aroused great interest among scientists for two reasons. First, it had now been established beyond doubt that life exists in deep water, contrary to the previous conclusion of Forbes that no life can occur below 300 fathoms. Second, the tiny stalked sea lily resembled in its structure some much larger animals hitherto known only from fossilized remains that had been found in rocks formed from ancient seabed sediments.

One English authority on sea lilies, W. B. Carpenter, expressed the opinion that *Rhizocrinus* is rather closely related to certain extinct sea lilies, or crinoids, of the Jurassic period. This would mean that the animal is related to life that flourished when the dinosaurs still existed, some 180 million years ago. Such comments triggered speculation that the hitherto unplumbed depths of the open oceans might prove to be a place of refuge for organisms which had supposedly become extinct millions of years before. The latter hypothesis was not justified by events, but the important discovery had been made that the deep ocean is indeed an abode of life and not an empty desert.

Other curious and mistaken ideas were dispelled one by one. Some scientists spoke of a mysterious zone in deep mid-water where all sunken ships, bodies of drowned sailors, and so on were supposed to remain suspended in water of density so great under pressure as to equal that of the items mentioned. Water is, in fact, almost incompressible, and objects sink to the floor of the deepest seas. Research ships not uncommonly dredge from great depths such items as beer cans thrown overboard from their own refuse the day before—and less commonly, objects thrown or fallen from passing ships two hundred years ago or more. All lie upon the seabed, and with them lie the teeth of sharks which shed them millions of years ago, and the hard petrosal bones of whales which lived and died ten thousand years ago.

The voyage of H.M.S. *Challenger,* in the 1870s—a major deep-sea exploring expedition—resulted in a great series of scientific reports, most of which are still in constant use, new editions appearing even in recent years. The expedition, which sampled the deep seas of most of the world from Arctic to Antarctic, marks the solid foundation of our present understanding of life in deep waters.

There is a certain irony about the meteoric growth of oceanography at this epoch, for in the light of after-knowledge we now perceive that the British scientists had apparently overlooked a significant discovery made as early as 1860 by Her Majesty's Ship *Bulldog.* In the course of a cruise performed in that year, the assistant engineer on board, named Steil, had invented an improvement in sounding machinery by means of which the vessel was able to recover about one pound of deep-sea mud from a depth of 2000 fathoms. Furthermore, one of the samples brought up from 1260 fathoms had yielded a sea star. Now, as we realize today, sea stars are among the most archaic animals surviving, and their extant members include representatives of forms of life which existed half a billion years ago, twice as ancient as existing crinoids, whose lineage seems to have begun in the Triassic period. Even the oldest extinct crinoids, from the Ordovician period, are no older than the oldest known kinds of sea stars. In other words, the *Bulldog* in 1860

had already disclosed the same kind of information as came from the lines of the Norwegian naturalist, but the scientific world was not then ready to appreciate this fact. Nor is that all. A careful review of British Admiralty archives reveals that Sir John Ross, working in Baffin Bay in the year 1816, had not only invented a clamshell-grab capable of bringing to the surface six pounds of sea-floor mud from a depth of 1000 fathoms, but also, using this device, he had actually recovered a living sea star from 800 fathoms. This event occurred eight years before Professor Forbes announced that no life exists in the sea below a depth of 300 fathoms.

By 1872 H.M.S. *Challenger* was ready to sail on what was to be her epoch-making cruise. Everyone was now talking, thinking, dreaming crinoids. Perhaps the most memorable day's dredging was July 14, 1874, off the Kermadec Isles north of New Zealand, when no fewer than eleven species of crinoid were taken from 600 fathoms. This was "probably the richest ground dredged by us at all," wrote Mosely afterward in 1879, when *Challenger* was once more back in British waters.

Extracts from letters and diaries convey something of the excitement and energy of the founders of modern oceanography. They also illustrate the international character of marine science, and the good personal relations that can develop between scientists of various nationalities. This aspect, happily, has always characterized the field, and has led to such successful programs as the so-called International Geophysical Year (1957–1959), the International Indian Ocean Expeditions of the 1960s, and comparable current programs. Despite international tensions, it has proved feasible for American, Russian, Japanese, British, French, Australian, and other expeditions to operate with friendly cooperation from other nations, and for their on-board scientists to develop rewarding friendships with their colleagues in other lands.

In the nineteenth century cable-laying ships recorded depths of eight kilometers in certain parts of the sea. More modern researchers have increased this figure to nearly eleven kilometers.

Modern soundings are made with the aid of echo sounders, which give a continuous recording along any transect followed by a ship. Thus very detailed topographic maps of the ocean bed are now becoming available at relatively little cost. Further still, the ability of sound waves of particular frequencies to penetrate the sediments of the sea floor, and to be reflected from the various discontinuities which occur between sediments of different consistencies, makes it possible for the echo sounder to yield charts showing the successive layers below the sea floor.

The painstaking measurements carried out by members of the *Challenger* expedition showed that the continental shelf slopes gradually down to an average depth of about 100 fathoms, then the seabed becomes steeper. This steeper part, known as the continental slope, plunges to about the average depth computed by Laplace, 2000 fathoms, and then becomes more nearly level. Actually, there are numerous submarine ridges and depressions. In some restricted regions, usually near land, the earth's crust seems to be thrown into great vertical folds, with deep trenches extending to depths of 5000 to 6000 fathoms.

Underwater photography by remote control, sampling by means of specially designed dredges and nets and, in more recent years, observations made from deep-sea submersibles such as the bathyscaphe, have all contributed to our better knowledge of the populations of animals that live at these great ocean depths.

Before the age of deep-sea exploration scientists had correctly inferred that no sunlight could reach these regions. They made one error, however, in supposing that there could be no life in the absence of an energy input from the sun. There is, in fact, a steady input of energy in several ways. One source of food is simply the bodies of organisms that have died in the upper sunlit layers of the sea. They drift downward toward the seabed and are eaten by the scavengers of the deep-water populations. Thus, even though there are no algae to trap energy from the sun, the deep-sea fauna ultimately derive energy from the activity of algae in the sunlit layers. Again, some of the mid-water animals rise to the surface at night, there to feed on upper-level organisms. Deeper down still are other layers of organisms that rise periodically into the overlying zones, there to attack and devour animals that have themselves preyed in a yet higher zone. So there is a vertical downflow of food and hence energy from upper layers to lower layers.

After the first deep-sea expeditions had succeeded in dredging and trawling actual samples of animals from the deepest layers of the sea and from the deepest parts of the floor of the sea, it became apparent that most of the denizens of the abyss are actually related to types of animals that live in the upper regions and on the continental shelf. So apparently these deep-sea fauna are derived from fauna of the upper regions. It seems as if at various times in the past animals of the upper regions had slowly migrated into deeper zones, there to adapt to altered conditions of life and to acquire the habit of feeding upon debris falling from the overlying waters, or to carry out periodic forays into the upper layers in order to snatch and carry downward suitable food animals that have become their prey. So, in spite of the belief that exploration of the deep sea might disclose surviving relics of ancient forms of life, as the early investigators had hoped, for the most part the conclusion is otherwise. Rather, the older forms of life are mainly still to be found on the continental shelf, if they have survived at all, and the denizens of the abyss are mostly of rather late origin, specialized for their peculiar mode of life in the deep.

NORTH ATLANTIC SEA LIFE

For many scuba divers the luxuriant underwater seascapes of tropical reefs remain an unattainable paradise, or one that can be visited at best only on rare occasions. For them the underwater experience is to be gained on coasts nearer home. The sections that follow deal with the temperate seas, beginning with the North Atlantic.

There are two principal types of coast—the rocky shoreline and the sandy beaches—and because the physical character of the seabed offers different kinds of living conditions in these two types of shore, the plants and animals that inhabit them are somewhat different. A rocky bottom, for example, offers a firm base for animals which attach themselves by suckers, such as sea anemones, or which cement their shells to the bottom, such as oysters. On the other hand, a sandy shore is suitable for animals which live buried in the bottom material, such as many clams and sea worms, whereas the hard boulder bottom or rock shelf prohibits these animals from gaining suitable resting places. However, rocky coasts commonly have headlands projecting out to sea, and this results in sheltered waters at the heads of the intervening bays. Silt or sand may accumulate in such sheltered places, making rocky coasts interesting places to visit, because of the contrasting type of environment often found not far away.

In all marine habitats the seaweeds form an important part of the community of organisms, because it is they that extract the energy from sunlight and store it as carbohydrates, the food of the browsing animals. Most of marine plant life is microscopic and not directly observable by the diver, though the small plankton animals that feed on the tiny floating one-celled plants are visible to the naked eye. For the benthic animals the larger seaweeds are more significant as food, and many of them can be seen creeping over the marine plants on which they browse.

Seaweeds (algae) are variously colored, depending on the presence of particular pigments used by the plant in synthesizing its organic materials from the dissolved nutrient salts that occur in seawater. One category of seaweeds are the green algae (Chlorophyta) in which the green pigment chlorophyll is conspicuously present. Like other seaweeds, the main body of the plant is a more or less flat, leaflike expansion called the thallus. Most commonly found in the mid-tidal region are various delicate and rather brightly tinted examples of the family Ulvaceae or sea lettuce, forming crinkly thin green expansions of thallus reminiscent of lettuce leaves. Two genera occur, a slightly thicker form with a double layer of cells in the thallus, called *Ulva* (commonest species *Ulva lactuca*), and a thinner, more delicate form with only a single layer of cells, now placed in a separate genus, *Monostroma.*

Much larger and more abundant are the leathery brown seaweeds called Phaeophyta or kelps, having a brown pigment (phaeophycin) as well as green chlorophyll in their tissues. In the mid-tidal region,

Punetaria forms a flat straplike brown thallus, about 5 to 20 centimeters long and about 1 to 2 centimeters wide, usually tapering at the tip, sometimes with the thallus bifurcated. It grows attached to the shells of mussels in intertidal rock pools. Another brown alga which grows on mussel shells in the same situation is *Scytosiphon lomentaria,* forming very slender grasslike filaments up to 20 centimeters long and a few millimeters wide.

A third category of seaweeds is formed by the *Rhodophyta* or Red Algae, growing mainly at depths below the lowest tidal level, though a few kinds, such as the purplish mosslike *Polysiphonia,* occur in the mid-tidal region. *Polysiphonia* is usually found growing attached to *Ascophyllum,* and any plant that has this habit of attaching itself to another plant is called an epiphyte.

Some other kinds of Rhodophyta become conspicuous at deeper levels below low tide, or where the bottom is only occasionally exposed at low tide. These include *Rhodymebia,* a red, fan-shaped expanded flat thallus, subdivided into about half a dozen bifurcated flat lobes, somewhat ragged at the extremity, the whole fan about 20 centimeters across, but the shape rather variable, sometimes more elongated and straplike. In the lower intertidal zone, and also in rock pools, a much smaller red seaweed occurs, about 6 centimeters across the frond, bifurcated several times, and of a purple-red color. This is *Chondrus crispus,* the edible sea dulse. Another red seaweed of this zone is the grasslike *Dumontia incrassata,* dark red when alive but fading to white on preservation or when cast ashore and dried up. A mosslike feathery seaweed is *Chondria,* found at a somewhat higher level, usually in rock pools; also *Porphyra,* closely resembling sea lettuce in shape and size, but differing conspicuously by its red-purple color.

The seaweeds comprise the herbage of the North Atlantic rocky shore environment. Ecologists recognize their importance, for they are the elements of the living population that generate the food material on which other organisms feed, namely the grazing animals. These seaweeds are analogous to the grass of land pastures. Herbivores comprise the next category of organisms, and they are analogous to herds of grazing animals.

(so far as oil spills permit), and the abalone stocks are increasing.

The west coast of North America yields fine examples of that ancient group of grazing sea snails called the keyhole limpets, family Fissurellidae. One species, *Megathura crenulata,* reaches 10 centimeters in length, about a hundred times larger than is usually the case with limpets of this group in other regions. Fissurellids have an aperture on the upper part of the shell for the ejection of fecal material. Of true limpets, family Acmaeidae, there is also a large west American species, namely *Lottia gigantea,* the owl limpet, reaching 10 centimeters in length. *Lottia* exhibits strong territorial behavior, driving off all intruders from an area of about one foot square upon the algae growth on which it feeds with the aid of its rasping tongue. Of the top shells, family Trochidae, the genus *Calliostoma* has species ranging from Alaska to San Diego (the genus also occurs in the southern hemisphere). *Tegula* is a common representative in the intertidal region.

The carnivorous mollusks that prey upon the herbivores here have as exuberant a development as do their prey. The trumpet whelks or Buccinidae, already noted in the North Atlantic fauna, occur here too. *Buccinum undatum* is lacking beyond the Arctic region, but there are some other notable species of this genus. Other genera of whelks familiar to the European and east American diver that also occur in the North Pacific include *Neptunea* and *Colos.*

The visitor from the North Atlantic will be surprised at the size and variety of North Pacific sea stars. A striking species is the many-armed sunflower sea star *Pycnopodia helianthoides,* which feeds on sea snails and often betrays this by irregular humps that appear on its body, marking the presence of undigested shells. In the north a large pentagonal sea star, *Patiria,* is common, and some five-armed species of *Pisaster,* covered by granules that impart a characteristic aspect. Farther south, toward the Mexican coast, the large tropical sea stars make their appearance, presenting a general similarity to those of the Gulf of Mexico, though the species are not the same.

The Crustaceans are numerous. The lobsters here belong to the genus *Panulirus,* lacking the enlarged claws of the Atlantic lobster, but resembling the rock lobster of Florida. A flattened kind of lobster, some-times called the prawnkiller, *Ibaccus,* and similar forms also occur. Crabs are abundant and varied in type, and so are their enemies, the octopuses.

On soft bottom, perhaps the most distinctive feature of the Pacific sea floors are the many kinds of flattened sea urchins called keyhole urchins and sand dollars. These all have a rigid shell and can easily be distinguished by this character from the venomous soft-shelled flattened sea urchins.

The very drastic seasonal temperature changes that afflict the northeast coast of New England and the Maritimes of Canada do not occur on the Pacific coasts of corresponding southern latitudes, so that the severe winterkill of New England marine animals does not occur there. Instead, the invertebrates, such as the snails, the sea stars, and sea urchins can live the whole year around in the rock pools, growing larger in each successive season and imparting a luxuriant aspect to the fauna. In contrast, the shore life of New England has to be replenished each spring by new immigrants from deeper water, to replace those that died the preceding winter when the sea froze at the surface. So the New England invertebrates do not, in general, grow as large as their relatives of British Columbia and California. This is perhaps the most striking feature a diver is likely to notice in the shallow-water faunas of the two coasts of northern North America. Deeper down, where different species live, ones not subject to the climatic changes, there is less difference between the same species.

THE SOUTHERN OCEANS

The overall productivity of the southern oceans is believed to be much lower than that of northern seas, though considerable uncertainties must exist so long as fishery exploitation of the southern seas remains mainly an offshore and inshore activity with only a few vessels engaged in fishing the open ocean. According to recent estimates, the Australian fishery yields only one-fortieth part of the annual catch on the coasts of the United States, although Australia has a coastline half as long again as that of the United States. The northern oceans at present yield about 95 percent of the world's annual fish catch. Although the number of fishing vessels operating in the southern seas is much less than in northern seas, there appear to be other, more fundamental reasons for the low catch. These probably include the following:

South of 30° south latitude, only 15 percent of the earth's surface is occupied by land, namely the southern half of Australia, New Zealand, and the southern extremities of South Africa and South America. The continental shelf regions of the southern oceans are accordingly very limited, and most food chains on which fishes depend are based on the bottom-dwelling invertebrates of the continental shelves. In contrast, the earth's surface, north of 30° north latitude, is 50 percent land, with a correspondingly higher area of continental shelf bottom. Thus the productivity of northern seas is greater. A second and more complicated reason for low productivity in the southern oceans is that most southern hemisphere coastlines lie in the warm-water belts of the ocean. Here the temperature layers of the ocean are more stable and do not suffer the drastic overturning of water masses that occur in the far northern seas. This, in turn, means that mineral-rich water from near the sea floor is not periodically brought to the surface the way it is in the northern seas, so the floating plant life of the southern oceans cannot gain access to the rich supplies of nutrients such as occur in the far north. This is turn lowers the production of grazing animals and, therefore, of fishes that prey upon the grazing animals.

Although the plankton of the southern oceans is less rich than that of the northern hemisphere, the life in waters close to land is abundant. On the coasts themselves there is usually a dense tangle of large seaweeds which provide food and shelter for the grazing animals and for the predators that feed on the grazing stock. These seaweeds include species larger than any known elsewhere in the world.

The well-known *Fucus* of the northern seas is here replaced by other somewhat similar brown seaweeds. On Australian and New Zealand coasts one of the most distinctive is *Hormosira* or Neptune's Necklace. The plants consist of strings of brown spherical hollow floats, joined in linear series like threaded beads. This olive-brown plant occurs at the level of the low tide and just below the average mid-tidal level. Here it forms very precise horizontal curtains on rocky shores, around the more sheltered coasts of southern Australia and New Zealand. Bladder-kelp, *Macrocystis pyrifera,* is a conspicuous seaweed on exposed rocky coasts. It grows in long ropelike masses up to 60 meters long, the central axis anchored to the rock holdfast on the bottom of the shelf by means of a robust rootlike lower termination. The free part of the axis slopes at an angle upward, rather like a fisherman's line, the angle determined by the direction and strength of the current. At intervals along the axis there are elliptical bladders, one at the base of each straplike branch of the huge thallus. The combined flotation power of all the hundreds of cysts serves to hold the whole plant in its erect posture. If a violent storm tears the plant away from the seabed, the thallus all floats to the surface to constitute a raft, capable of drifting thousands of miles, and of carrying miniature ecosystems of benthic and epiphytic organisms, plus a cloud of kelp-fishes underswimming the whole. Sometimes the algae become entangled with a log or logs, and with other species of kelp, in which case rafts of up to 15 meters in diameter can be produced.

The largest kelps in the world, giants of their kind, are the several species of brown bull kelp, of the genus *Durvillea.* One of the best known is *Durvillea antarctica* which, despite its name, also ranges the temperate seas of the southern hemisphere. The body of the seaweed, the so-called thallus, incorporates the flotation chambers within its own substance, like a pith inside the leathery straplike masses.

The drifting rafts formed by these great brown seaweeds have played an important role in distributing marine benthos from one side of the ocean to the other. The distances between the southern continents are far greater than between the continents of the northern hemisphere, so fewer genera and species are shared by the southern continents, for the transoceanic passage is so much more difficult. When one compares the forms that are shared, however, it is soon apparent that they comprise just those types of animal and plant that might be expected to traverse the ocean successfully.

One piece of evidence lies in the distribution of the

giant kelps themselves. These occur along the southern coasts of all the southern continents. They have been observed drifting at sea in raft formation, so there can be little doubt that this is the manner in which they have achieved their present circumpolar dispersion.

A second piece of evidence lies in the habits of the animals that have achieved a corresponding circumpolar distribution. For these animals, though living on the seabed and forming no part of the drifting plankton, have nevertheless apparently drifted across the southern oceans, to establish colonies on the southern coasts of South America, Southern Australia, and New Zealand. South Africa is usually omitted from the sequence of colonization, because it lies in the subtropical belt and is not strictly involved in the westwind-drift system of the southern hemisphere.

One of the genera of sea stars that evidently dispersed by means of rafting across the South Pacific Ocean is *Allostichaster*, with species in New Zealand and South America. It is well adapted to making such a crossing, for it inhabits the shore zone where large floating kelp occurs, and it has the power of asexual reproduction by the simple process of dividing in half. Thus a raft need carry only one accidental passenger of either sex, not two passengers representing both sexes. The one solitary voyager is enough to establish a new colony on a remote island or coast.

Calvasterias is another sea star that ranges both sides of the South Pacific. Here the factor that favors the transfer is the female's habit of carrying her brood for about six months, which means that one pregnant female can establish a new colony. One genus of sea urchins is distributed on coasts of South America, South Australia, and New Zealand, as well as on various island groups in mid-ocean between these continents. Here, it is apparently the small size of the urchin that has favored its accidental rafting on board kelp.

In a different category of transoceanic voyagers are the large southern rock lobsters of the genus *Jasus*. These occur on all southern continents, including South Africa, though not in Antarctica, where the climate is too severe. They occur also on various intervening island groups. Their means of transfer is apparently transoceanic planktonic dispersal, for the larval stages are long-lived floating forms, liberated in large numbers from the hatching eggs each year. It is thought likely that much of the Australian brood is swept to sea by the west-wind-drift, to come to land on the New Zealand coast. It is possible, though not proven, that the New Zealand progeny are similarly swept to sea to make an eventual landfall in South America.

Lampreys are fishlike animals that have no paired fins. The adult lampreys ascend streams to lay the eggs in fresh water, where the young stages are passed. Lampreys of one species, *Geotria australis*, have been found to occur in rivers in Australia, New Zealand, and South America. At first this suggested that the southern continents must at one time have been joined, for it was considered that freshwater fish could not possibly cross oceans. Then, during the International Geophysical Year, the same species was discovered in the Antarctic Ocean. Now it is realized that the southern lamprey spends part of its adult life at sea, making its circumpolar distribution quite feasible.

A similar explanation has now been found for the circumpolar distribution of southern fishes called galaxiids. These, too, occur in South America, Australia, and New Zealand, in rivers and lakes. And these, too, were taken to be a justification for the theory that the southern continents were once all joined. Now it is known that only the adult stages are spent in rivers and lakes. The young stages live in the sea, and the life history resembles that of salmon in the northern hemisphere. Obviously the circumpolar distribution has been achieved by transoceanic dispersion in the immature state while living in the sea.

Apart from these special features of southern hemisphere marine life, southern marine organisms in general are very similar to those of the north. There is, indeed, an underlying unity in our perception of the associations of living beings that comprise the fauna and flora of the seas, whether of the tropics, of the two northern oceans, or of the great southern seaway that girdles our planet.

GLOSSARY

ABYSS   The sea floor below the continental slope, having an average depth of 4 kilometers or 2.5 miles. Most of the seabed constitutes the abyss.

ALCYONARIAN   Type of coral in which there are eight tentacles and the skeleton is composed of spicules of lime imbedded in hornlike material; they are commonly colored red or orange and include the sea whips and sea fans.

AMPHIPOD   Type of small crustacean resembling a large flea, the most common kinds being the sand hoppers.

ANTHOZOA   Group of marine invertebrates comprising anemones and corals.

ANTIPATHARIAN   Type of coral secreting a black skeleton, forming treelike colonies, mainly in deep water, not forming reefs.

ANTITRADES   Oceanic winds, blowing mainly from west to east, occurring in temperate latitudes; see *West-wind-drift, Roaring Forties*.

APERTURE   The opening in a gastropod shell through which the snail emerges.

ASEXUAL   Stage in the life history or mode of reproduction in which young are produced by budding and not by the production of sex cells.

ASTEROID   Member of the echinoderm class Asteroidea, the sea stars.

ATOLL   Ring-shaped coral reef formed from a fringing reef of an island that has subsequently sunk beneath the sea.

BARNACLE   Member of the crustacean class Cirripedia. All barnacles are marine and sedentary in the adult stage.

BASKET STAR   A brittle star of the echinoderm class Ophiuroidea, having arms that fork several times, simulating a mesh basket.

BATHYMETRIC RANGE   A statement giving the minimum and maximum depths at which an organism may be found living.

BENTHOS   The sea-floor organisms taken collectively, as opposed to swimming or floating marine organisms.

BIOCHROME   An organic pigment found in echinoderms and some other animals.

BIVALVE   A member of the molluscan class Bivalvia, the clams, in which the shell forms two hinged parts.

BRITTLE STAR   A star-shaped, long-armed echinoderm in which the arms are very flexible and formed from numerous similar joints. Class Ophiuroidea.

CARBOHYDRATE   An organic compound of carbon, hydrogen, and oxygen, such as sugar or starch, formed by plants and required as a food substance by animals.

CENTIMETER (cm)   Metric unit of length, about two-fifths of an inch, and 0.01 meter.

CEPHALOPODS   The octopuses and squids, forming the molluscan class Cephalopoda.

CHITON   A mollusk of limpet-like aspect, usually with eight shelly plates, forming a distinct class of mollusks called the Amphineura.

CHLOROPHYTA   The green seaweeds, found mainly in shallow water.

CIRRIPEDIA   A class of crustaceans comprising the barnacles.

CONTINENTAL SHELF   The seabed from shoreline to a depth of about 100 fathoms or 200 meters (about 600 feet), extending out to sea until the angle of slope of the seabed increases at the continental slope (which see).

CONTINENTAL SLOPE   The outer margin of a continental mass, where the depth of the seabed drops from the edge of the continental shelf down to the abyss. See *abyss, continental shelf*.

COPEPOD   A small planktonic crustacean used as food by fishes and other animals.

CRINOIDEA   A class of echinoderms comprising sea lilies and feather stars.

CRUSTACEA   A large assemblage of segmented invertebrates with a hard jointed outer integument and jointed limbs; includes crabs, lobsters, and similar animals.

CTENOPHORA   A group of gelatinous plankton animals, related to jellyfishes but having special swimming organs called combs; active carnivores.

DECAPODA (1)   A group of crustaceans having five pairs of walking or swimming limbs, comprising crabs and lobsters.

DECAPODA (2)   The ten-armed members of the Cephalopoda, comprising squids.

DEEP   Term used for any unusually deep part of the abyss, and also for any trench; see *abyss, trench.*

DIATOM   A type of one-celled floating or bottom-dwelling plant in which the living cell is enclosed in two silica valves. Diatoms are the most abundant plants in the ocean and serve as food for many small animals.

DOMINANT   Term used as a noun for any taxon that is so conspicuous in a living community as to give its name to the community; see *subdominant.* For example, the brittle star *Amphiura* is the dominant genus of the *Amphiura-Echinocardium* community on muddy sea floors.

ECHINODERMATA   A group (phylum) of marine animals comprising the sea stars, the sea urchins, sea cucumbers, and sea lilies.

ECHINOID   A sea urchin; see *Echinodermata.*

ECOLOGY   The study of animals and plants in relation to their environment.

ECOSYSTEM   Any self-maintaining combination of plants and animals together with their environment. The *marine ecosystem* comprises the oceans, the marine fauna and flora, together with the energy input from sunlight.

ELASMOBRANCHS   The sharks and rays, cartilaginous fishes that have louver-like gill openings.

EOCENE PERIOD   A former epoch in the earth's history extending from about 60 to 50 million years ago.

EPIFAUNA   That part of the benthos living on the visible surface of the seabed.

EQUATORIAL CURRENTS   The mainly east-to-west currents of warm water that lie in the tropics north and south of the equator. These currents are driven by the trade winds (which see).

FAUNA   The entire range of species of animals in a particular region.

FATHOM   Six feet, or roughly 2 meters, a measure of depth.

FILTER FEEDER   An aquatic animal that obtains minute food particles by filtering seawater. An example is an oyster, or a sponge.

FLORA   The entire range of species of plants in a particular region.

FOOD CHAIN   The sequence of organisms in which each member to the left serves as food to the member immediately to the right. An example of a food chain is Diatoms-Copepods-Herring-Tuna-Swordfish-Man. Toxic pollutants that cannot be excreted pass along the chain from left to right and become concentrated in the right-hand members.

FOOD WEB   A more complex form of food chain in which various lateral branches occur where several organisms lie at the same levels on the chain.

GENUS   The first part of a binomial name of a plant or animal, of which the second part is the species. Thus the oyster *Ostrea edulis* is one particular species *(edulis)* of the genus *Ostrea,* and *Ostrea ingens* is another species of the same genus. Generic names are capitalized, specific names are not capitalized. Both generic and specific names are always written in italics, by an international convention.

GROWTH LINES   Successive increments of growth of a tissue or shell, indicative of a time span during which growth has occurred. Growth lines in corals are important indicators of ancient astronomical information, such as the rate at which the earth rotated in former epochs, and former distances of the moon from the earth (see section "Reef Corals").

HEART URCHIN   A kind of sea urchin in which the body is heart-shaped, known technically as spatangoids, and inhabiting mud and silt as infauna.

HERMIT CRAB   Any member of the decapod Orustacea having the habit of occupying discarded shells of sea snails.

HETEROPODA   Planktonic sea snails with a colorless body.

HEXACORALS   The corals with six-part symmetry, secreting a limy skeleton.

HOLOTHURIAN   A sea cucumber, a member of the Echinodermata.

HYDROCORAL   A fire coral, a hydrozoan secreting a stony skeleton.

HYDROZOAN   Usually small animal related to jellyfishes and sea anemones but differing from both in having alternating generations of free-swimming and sedentary adult stages. A few hydrozoans are able to secrete a lime skeleton; see *hydrocoral.*

ISOPODS   Mainly small flattened crustaceans resembling pill bugs.

JURASSIC PERIOD   Epoch in earth history extending from 160 to 120 million years ago.

KILOMETER (km)   Metric unit of length, approximately 0.6 mile, equal to 100 meters. The average depth of the sea is 4 kilometers or 2.5 miles.

LAGOON   The shallow sheltered sea within an atoll or behind a barrier reef.

LARVA   An immature developmental stage. Larvae of marine animals are often planktonic.

LOBSTER   Large decapod crustacean in which the abdomen is not folded under the thorax. The large North Atlantic lobster, *Homarus,* has pincerlike front claws; lobsters of the tropics, North and South Pacific, and southern seas lack the enlarged claws.

METER (m)   Metric unit of length, about 39 inches.

MIOCENE   Epoch in earth history extending from about 25 to 10 million years ago.

MOLLUSCA   A large assemblage of invertebrates comprising the chitons, sea snails, clams, octopuses, and squids, together with a few other lesser-known types.

MYSTICETI   A group of whales (Cetacea) in which horn plates or baleen form a filter-feeding sieve around the jaws.

NAUPLIUS   The youngest larval stage of a crustacean, usually a free-swimming planktonic stage, and sometimes the only evidence that an animal belongs to the phylum Crustacea (as in parasitic barnacles).

NEKTON   Collective name for all swimming marine animals; see *plankton, benthos.*

NOMINAL SPECIES   Name used for an animal or plant about which insufficient information is available to determine its exact affinity.

NUDIBRANCH   A sluglike free-swimming or creeping sea snail that lacks a shell and usually carries a tuft of soft appendages called cerata, and in which the body is often brightly colored. The cerata are used as offensive organs and are armed with stinging cells obtained from sea anemones and related animals.

OCTOPODA   A group of cephalopod mollusks having eight suctorial arms, the octopuses.

ODOBAENIDAE   The walruses, a family of Pinnipedia.

ODONTOCETI   The toothed whales and dolphins, of the order Cetacea.

OPHIUROIDEA   The brittle stars, a group of echinoderms.

ORDOVICIAN   Period in earth history extending from about 500 to 460 million years ago.

OTARIIDAE   A group of Pinnipedia known as the eared seals.

PALOLO WORM   A name applied to various species of bristle worm that have strong lunar periodicity in reproduction and can be captured for use as food at times related to the phase of the moon.

PEDICELLARIA   Minute pincer-shaped defensive organ, sometimes venomous, found in large numbers on the skin of some echinoderms.

PERIODICITY   Regularly repeated behavior, such as sexual activity, coordinated with some other factor, such as phases of the moon.

PHAEOPHYTA   The brown seaweeds, including laminarians or kelps.

PHOCIDAE   The family name of the true seals, in which the external ears are not visible.

PHOTOSYNTHESIS   Chemical process by which plants convert carbon dioxide and water into carbohydrates in the presence of sunlight and chlorophyll (or other pigment).

PHYLUM   Name of the major natural groupings of plants and animals; plural *phyla.* Examples of phyla are Chlorophyta, Mollusca.

PINNIPEDIA   Marine carnivores comprising the walruses, eared seals, and true seals.

PLANKTON   Collective name for all floating marine organisms.

PLANULA   The free-swimming larval stage of hydrozoans and jellyfishes.

PLUTEUS   The free-swimming larval stage of sea urchins and brittle stars.

POLAR WANDERING THEORY   Concept that the earth's poles of rotation have changed their positions through time. See section "Reef Corals."

POLYCHAETA   The bristle worms.

POLYP   The anchored stage resembling a sea anemone occurring during the life history of hydrozoans and jellyfishes; also the corresponding (and only) phase in the life history of sea anemones and corals.

PORIFERA   The phylum name of sponges.

PREDATOR   An animal that obtains food by preying upon other animals. In a food chain the predators are placed to the right of the grazing animals; see *food chain, ecosystem.*

PROTEINS   Organic compounds produced by plants and animals, containing carbon, hydrogen, oxygen, and nitrogen, the basis of living tissues.

PTEROPODS   Name given to two groups of free-swimming and floating sea snails often brightly colored, found in large schools in the open sea, commonly called sea butterflies.

REGENERATION   The power of many marine invertebrates to restore lost organs.

REGULARIA   Name given to the group of sea urchins in which the body has a rounded shape; most live on hard bottom.

RHODOPHYTA   The red seaweeds, including the corallines or nullipores of coral reefs and also cold-water forms that can live far out on the continental shelf, below the level at which other seaweeds can live.

ROARING FORTIES   Mariners' name for southern latitudes bordering the 40° S parallel, in which the antitrades are strong and unremitting, producing the current called the west-wind-drift; see *antitrades.*

SCATTERING LAYER   A horizontal layer of floating or swimming animals, producing a so-called scattering effect on the signal of sonar sounding devices. Different species produce the effect at different depths, depending on the time of day. See section "The Mysterious Deep." Animals of the scattering layers acquire food at higher levels and transfer it to greater depths, hence compensating for the lack of sunlight energy in the deep sea.

SCAPHOPODA   Small group of mollusks that have a shell shaped like a tusk.

SCYPHOZOA   Group name applied to all jellyfishes.

SEINE   A fishing net like a series of tennis-court nets strung end to end, with floats along the top edge and weights along the bottom, to hold the net vertical. Known to the ancient Egyptians, and still used today.

SHELF   Oceanographers' abbreviation for *continental shelf,* (which see).

SIPHON   Suctorial organ of feeding found in predatory mollusks; also used for tubular organs that carry a current of water in filter-feeding animals such as clams and tunicates.

SIPHONOPHORA   Group name applied to planktonic colonial hydrozoans such as the Portuguese man-of-war, *Physalia.*

SOMALI CURRENT   An oceanic current to the northeast of Africa in which the direction of flow reverses seasonally, in sympathy with the reversing monsoon winds, important therefore in proving that ocean currents are produced by oceanic winds.

SPATANGIDS   The heart-shaped sea urchins, usually found living on or imbedded in soft mud or sand on the sea floor and the lagoons of atolls. To be contrasted with *Irregularia,* (which see).

SPECIES   Name applied to any single kind of plant or animal of which all the individuals form a breeding group. For comments on the accepted use of the word, see *genus.*

SPIRE   The pointed posterior part of the shell of a sea snail.

STILLSTAND   An inferred halt in changes of sea level, during which the ocean remains at a fixed level when climatic change is temporarily suspended. During stillstands the waves cut platforms on rocky coasts; such platforms or terraces are evidence of former stillstands, and are found on the seabed and on terrain above present sea level, showing that the ocean has stood at various heights in the past. High sea levels occur during warm climatic phases, when the polar ice melts; low sea levels occur during ice ages.

SUBDOMINANT   Term used for a species that is conspicuous in a community, though not so conspicuous as the *dominant,* (which see). In the *Amphiura-Echinocardium* community, for example, the second named genus yields the subdominant species. The use of dominants and subdominants in these contexts is merely a convenient way of attaching an identifying label to a community.

TAXON   Any grouping of like plants or animals to which a single name can be applied, and which can be defined by a shared character or characters. Examples of taxa are *species* (in which all included individuals are similar); any *genus* (in which all included species share some common characters); any *family* (in which all included genera share some common characters)—and so on.

TRADE WINDS   Name applied to the steady easterlies that blow across all oceans between the latitudes of 30° N and 30° S. The trade winds drive the equatorial currents that flow from east to west. See *antitrades.*

TRAWL   A bag-shaped net dragged along the sea floor, or trailed through mid-water, invented by the ancient Egyptians and still used today. See *seine.* Still the principal sampling device in deep water, but scuba diving has partly replaced the trawl in shallow waters.

TRENCH   The deepest folds in the oceanic sea floor, some extending to depths of nearly 7 miles, or 11 kilometers.

TROPICOPOLITAN OR PANTROPICAL   Terms used to describe organisms that range all tropical seas, such as the sea star *Linckia guildingii.* It is inferred that such species must date back to geological periods when the major oceans were interconnected by seaways located in the tropical zone. See section "Echinoderms of Coral Reefs."

TUNICATES   Filter-feeding marine animals that secrete an outer leathery or glassy protective sheath, the tunic, and which sometimes have a fishlike larval stage. Salps are planktonic tunicates; sea squirts are benthic members.

WAVE-CUT PLATFORM   A horizontal terrace cut by wave action into coastlines during stillstands (which see).

WEST-WIND DRIFT   The eastward-flowing current produced in temperate regions by the passage across the ocean of the antitrade winds (which see).

WHELK   A trumpet-shaped sea snail. The term is usually restricted to those with a siphon (which see), and hence with carnivorous habits. The northern genus *Buccinum* is a typical whelk.

ZOAEA   A peculiar free-swimming larval stage of crabs and lobsters, having a disproportionately large head and long bristles used as flotation aids.

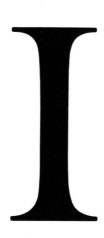

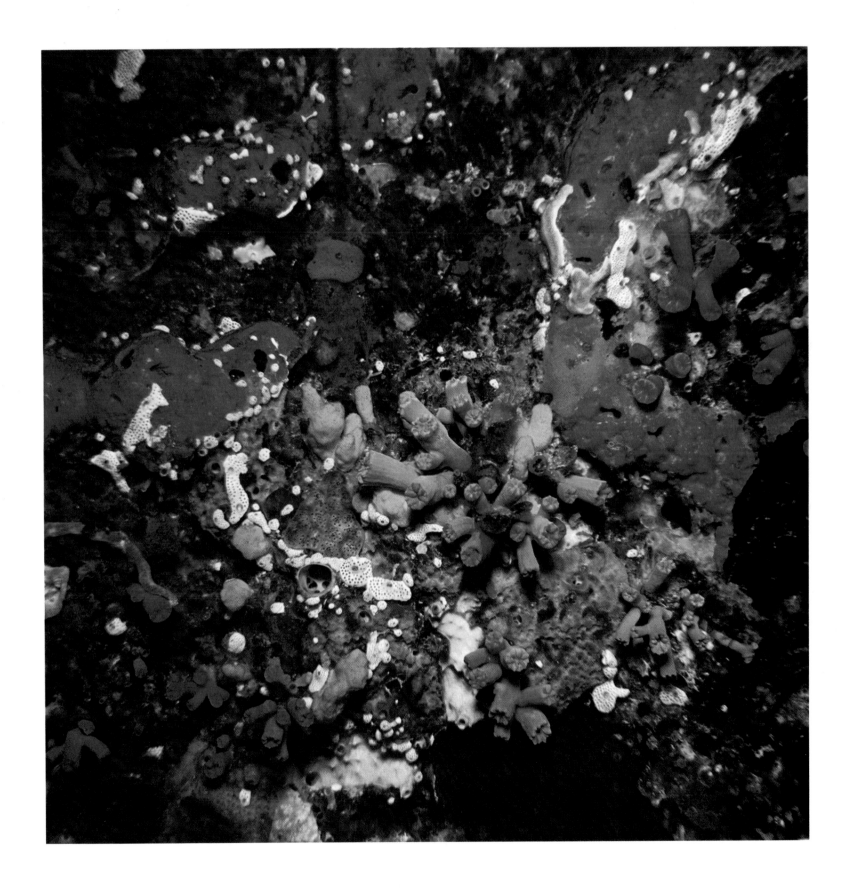

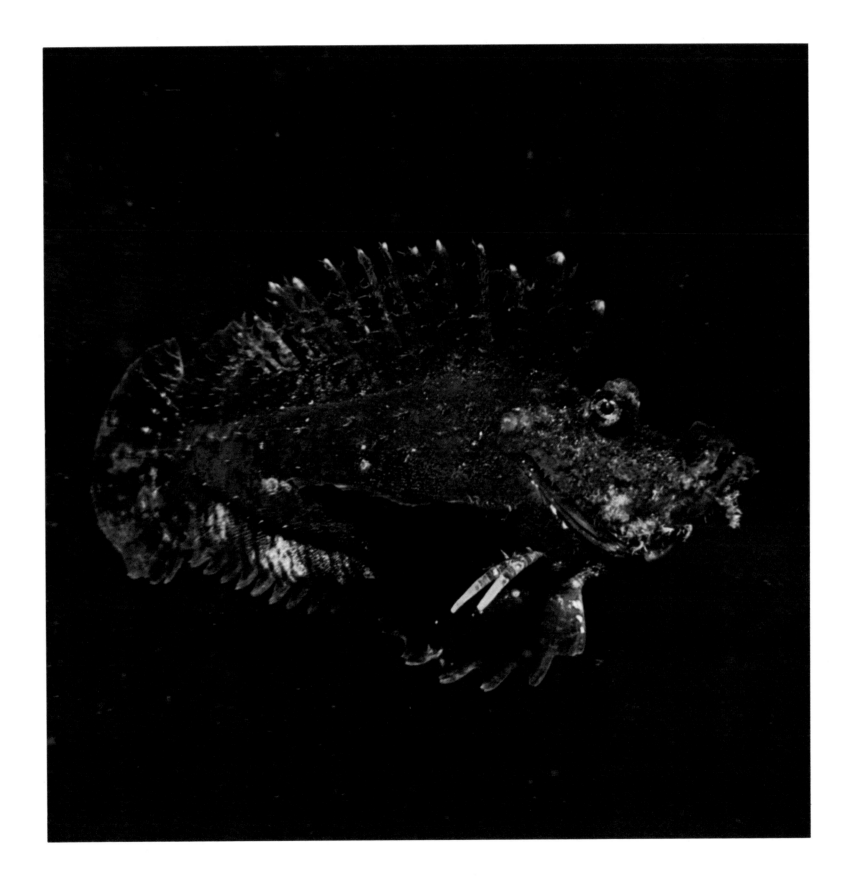

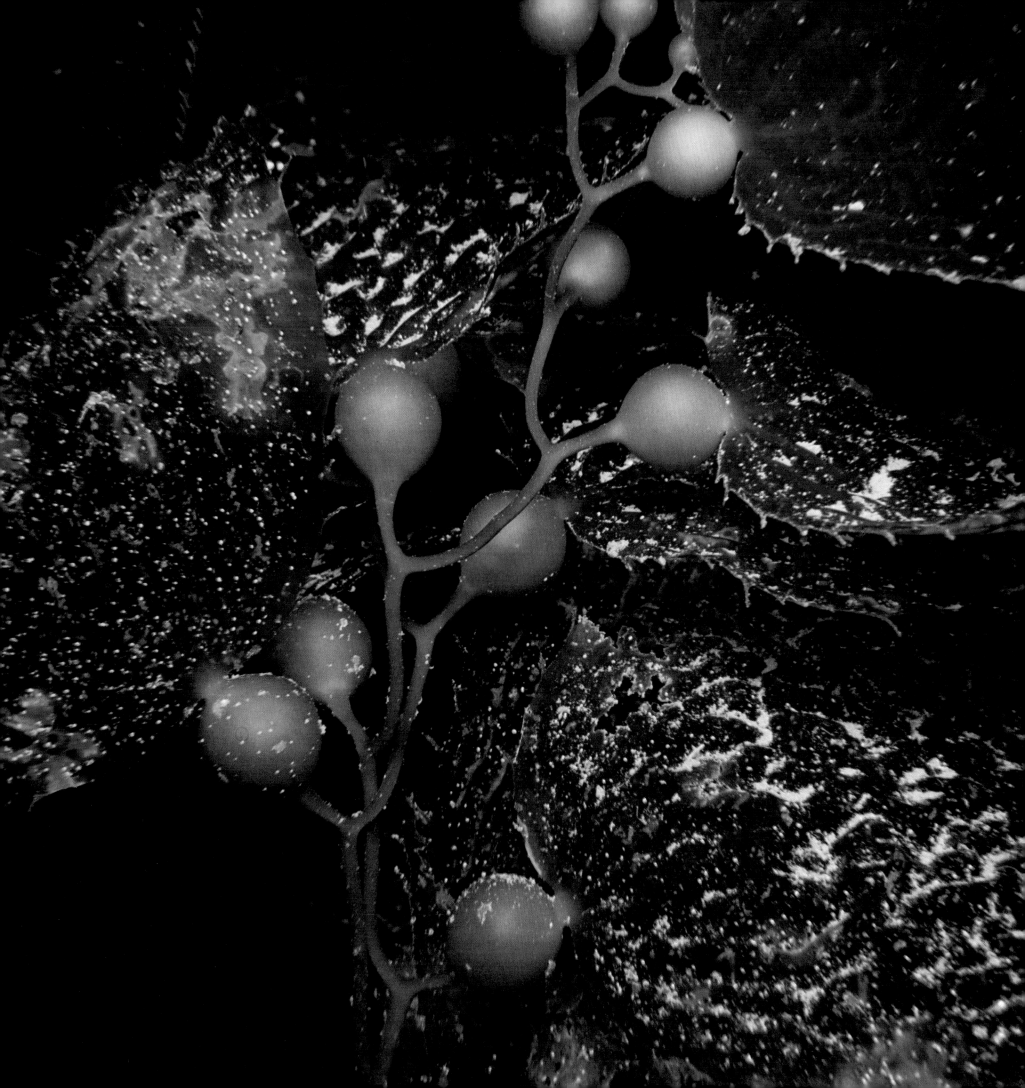

II

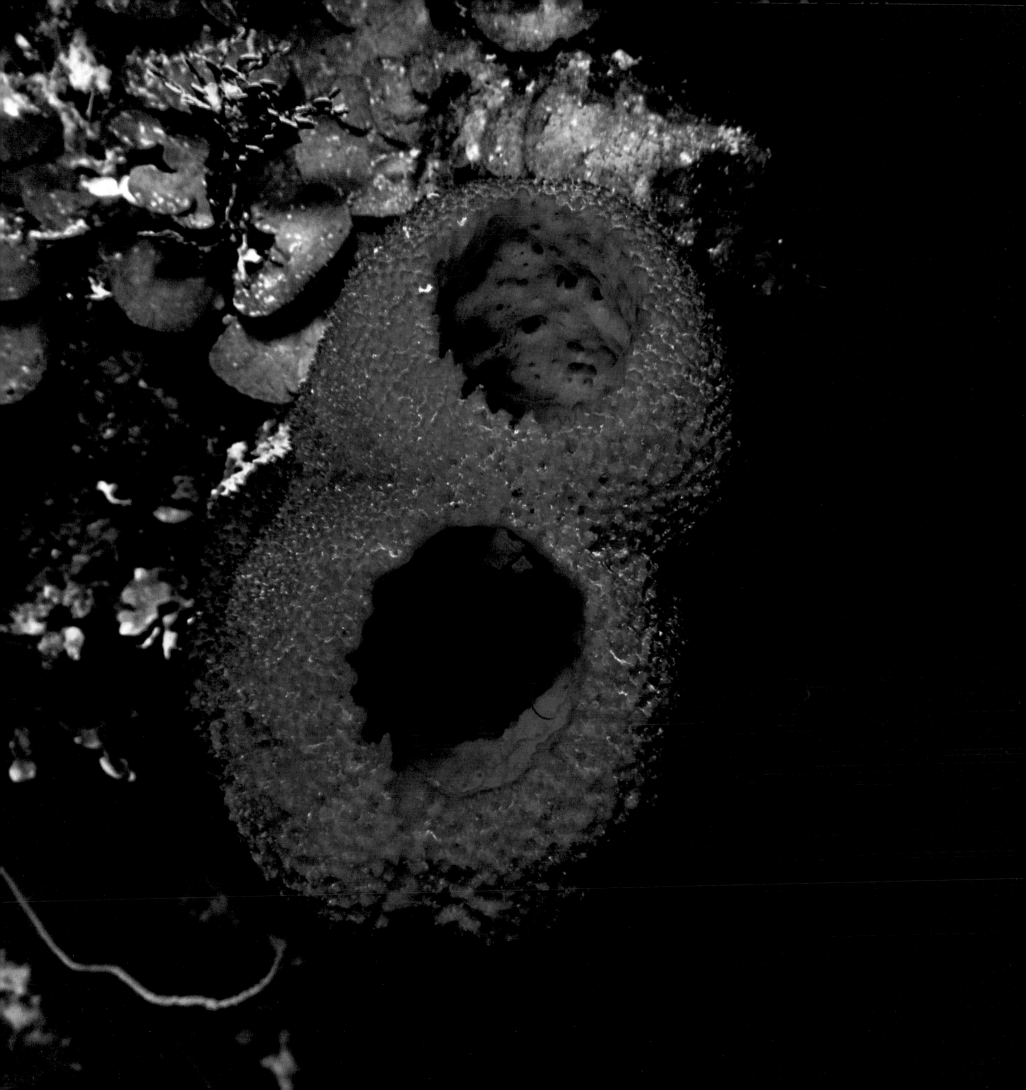

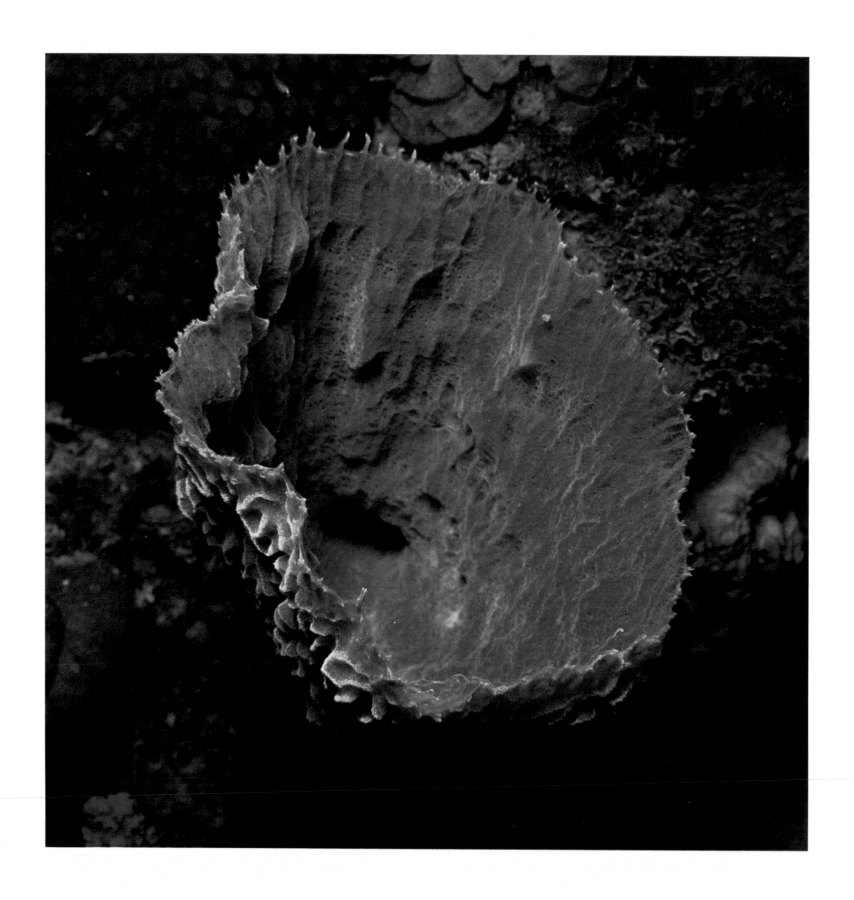

III

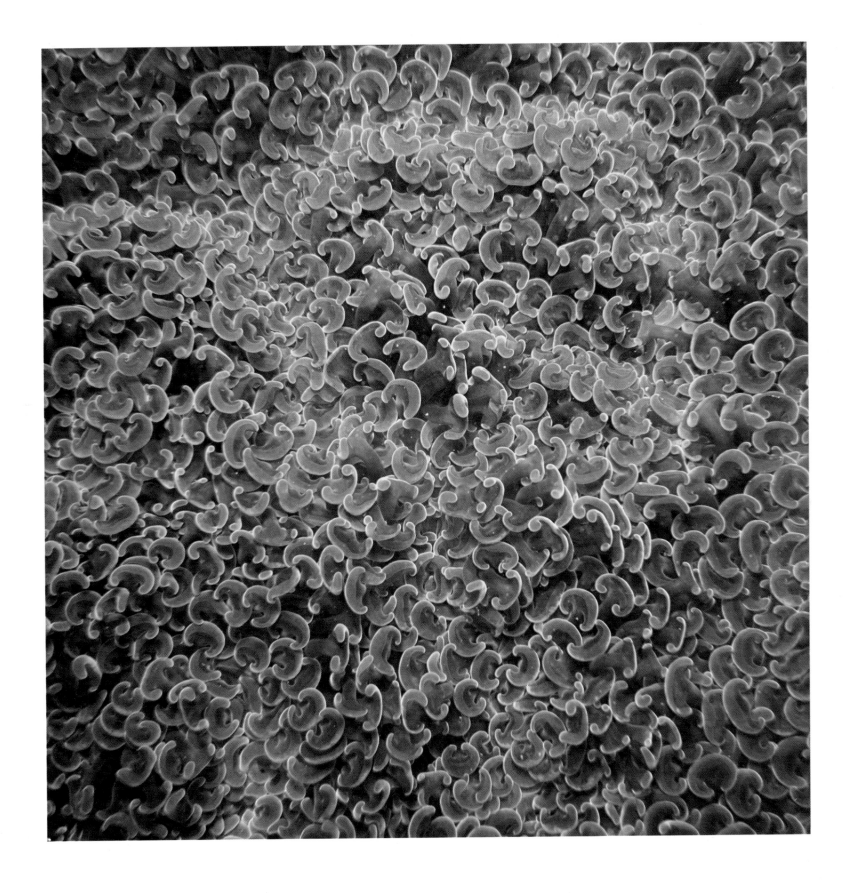

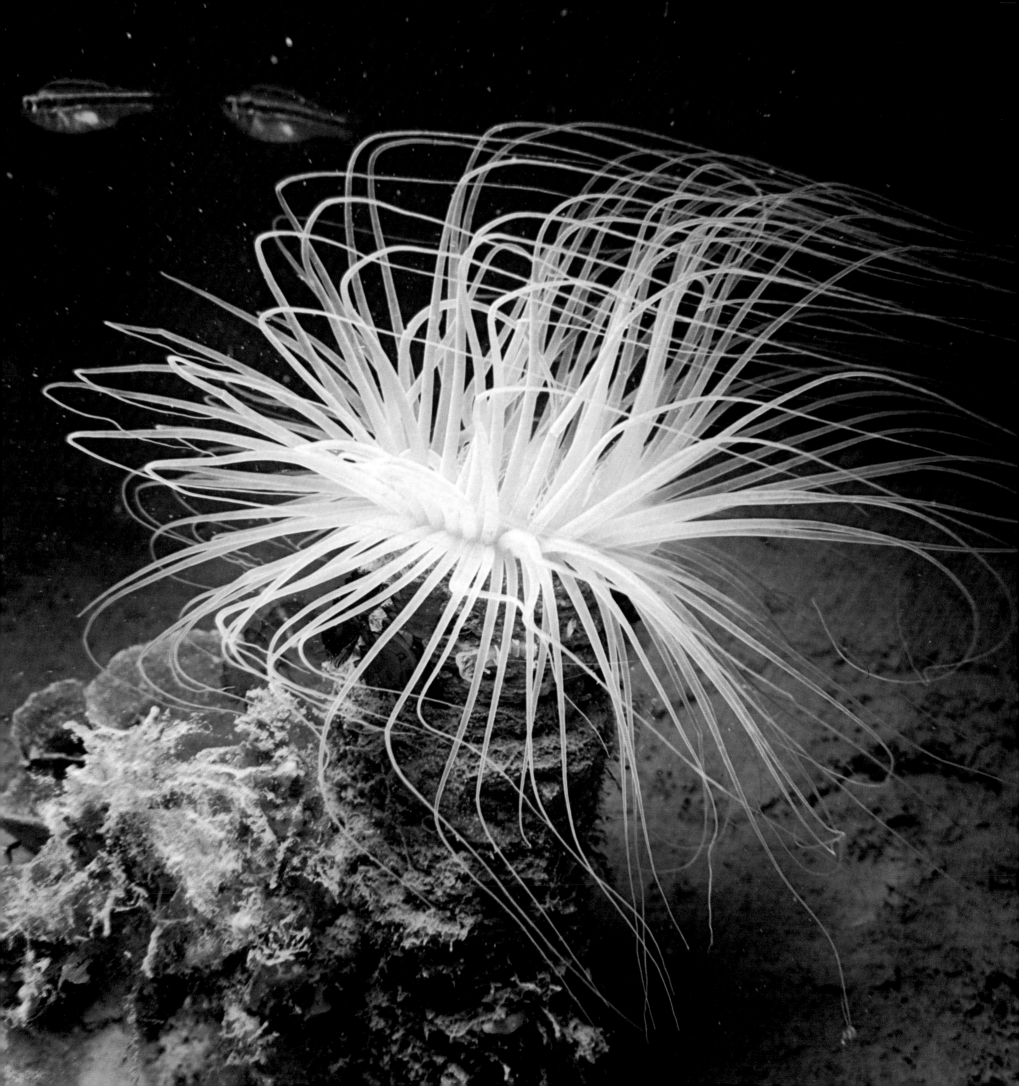

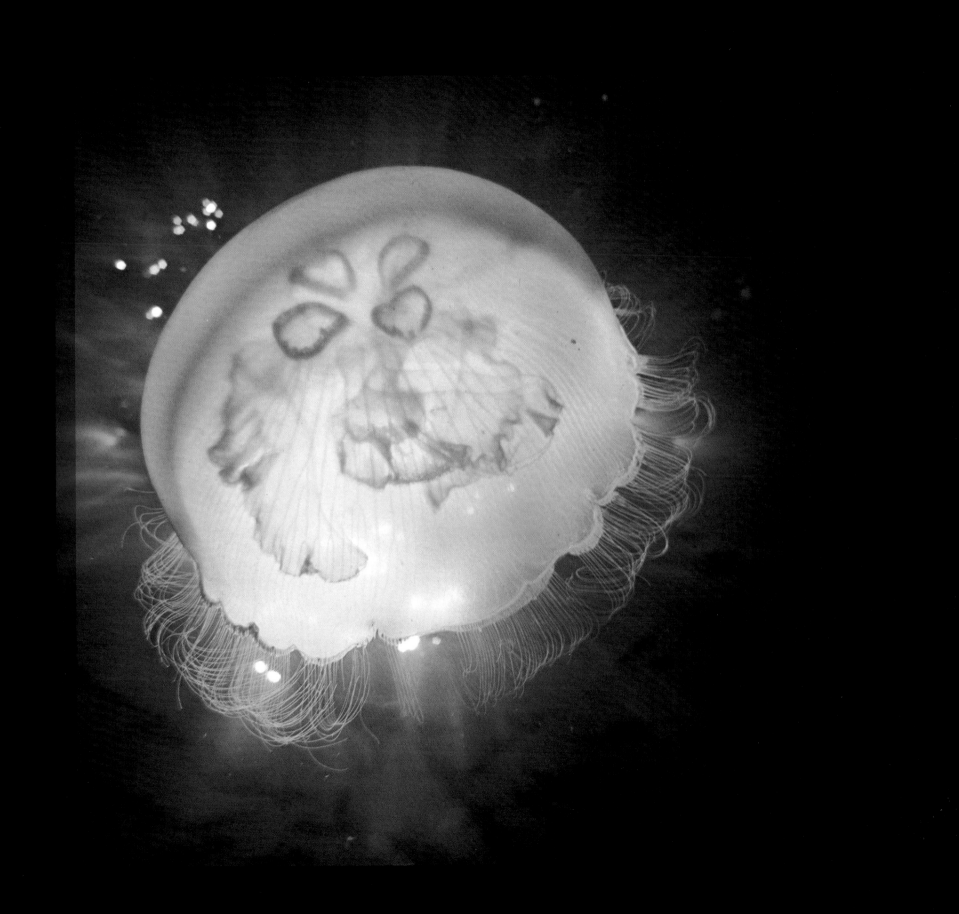

IV

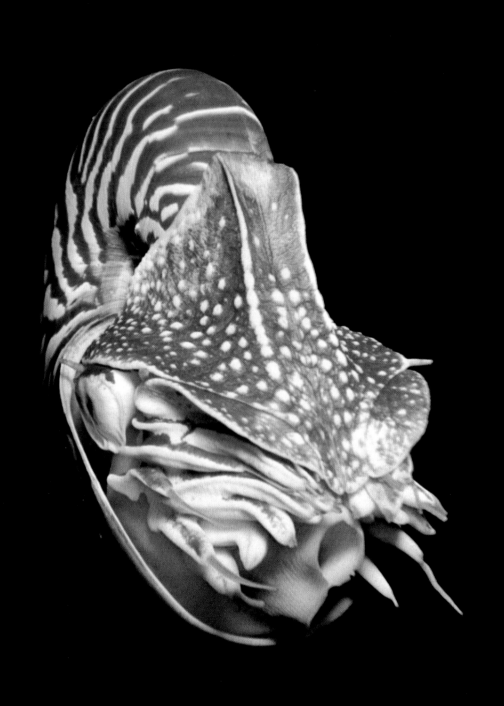

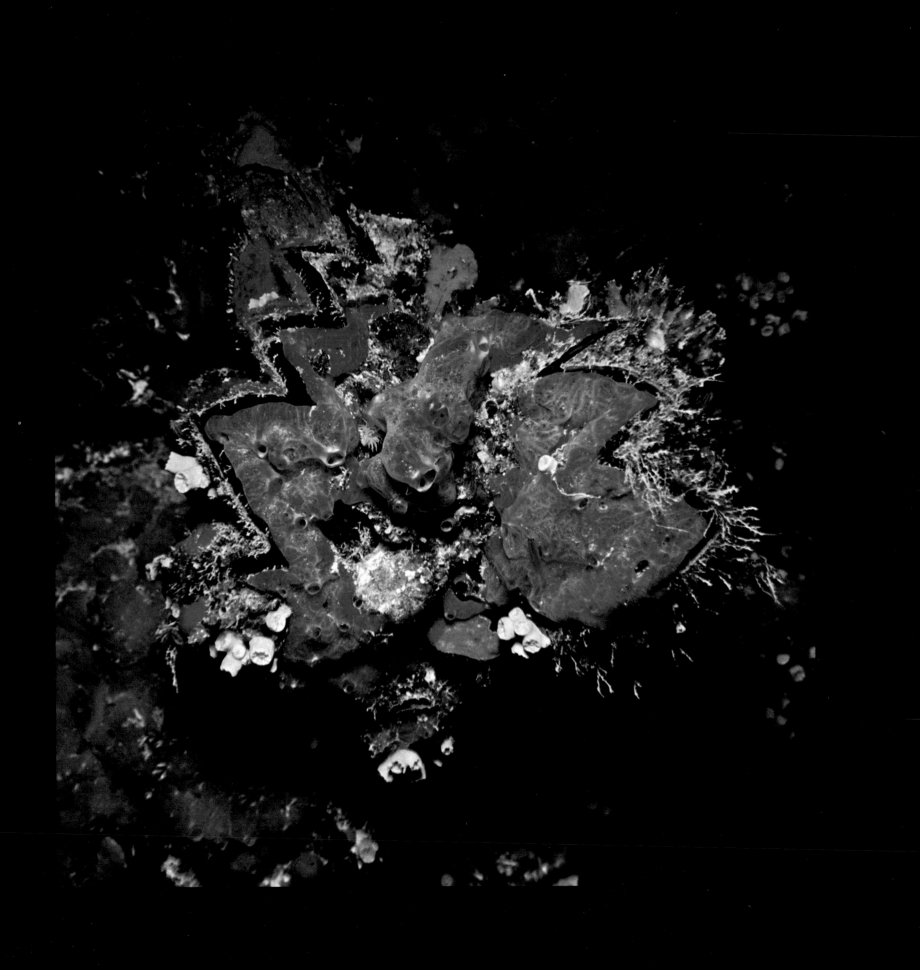

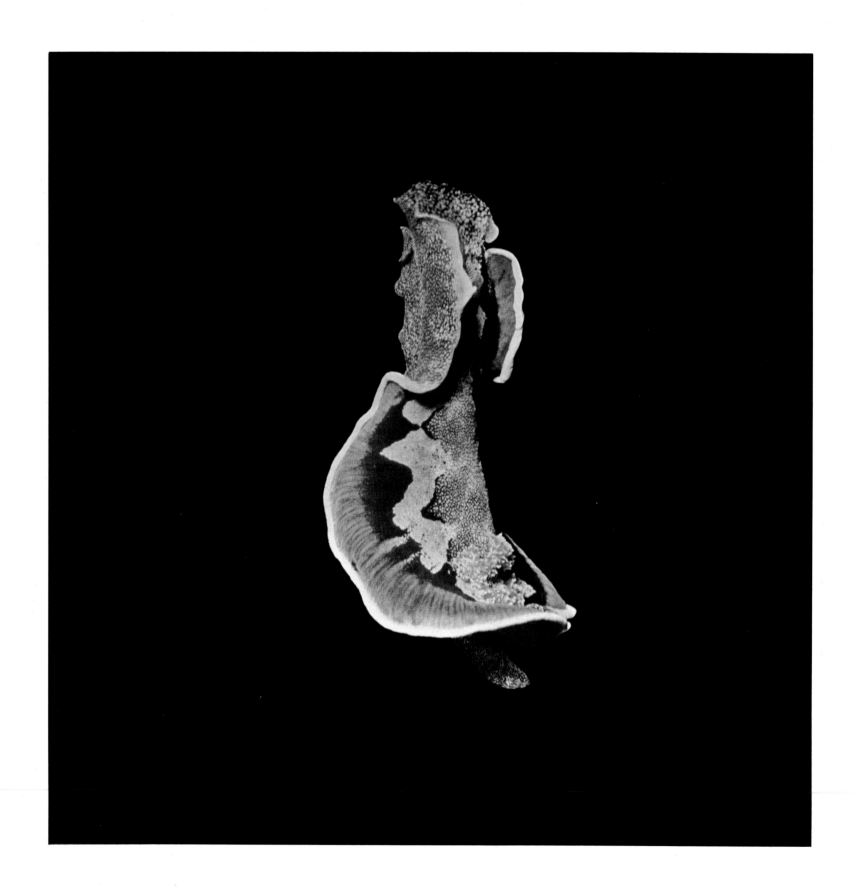

VI

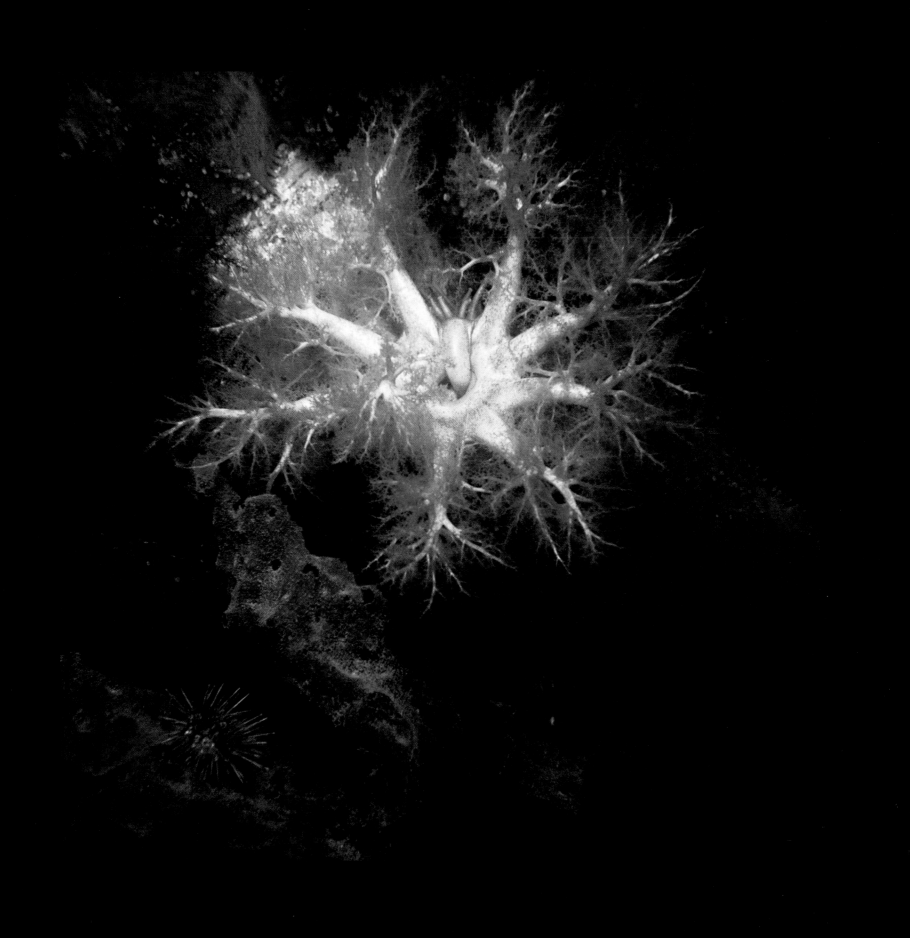

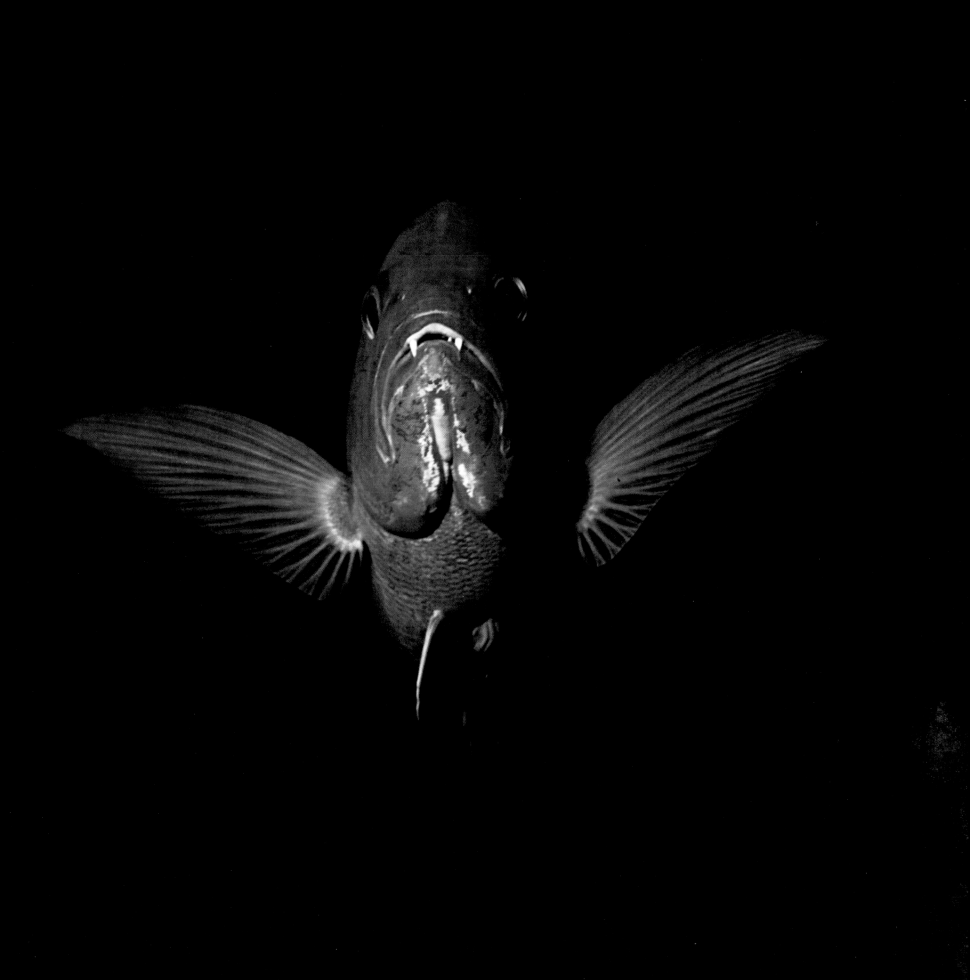

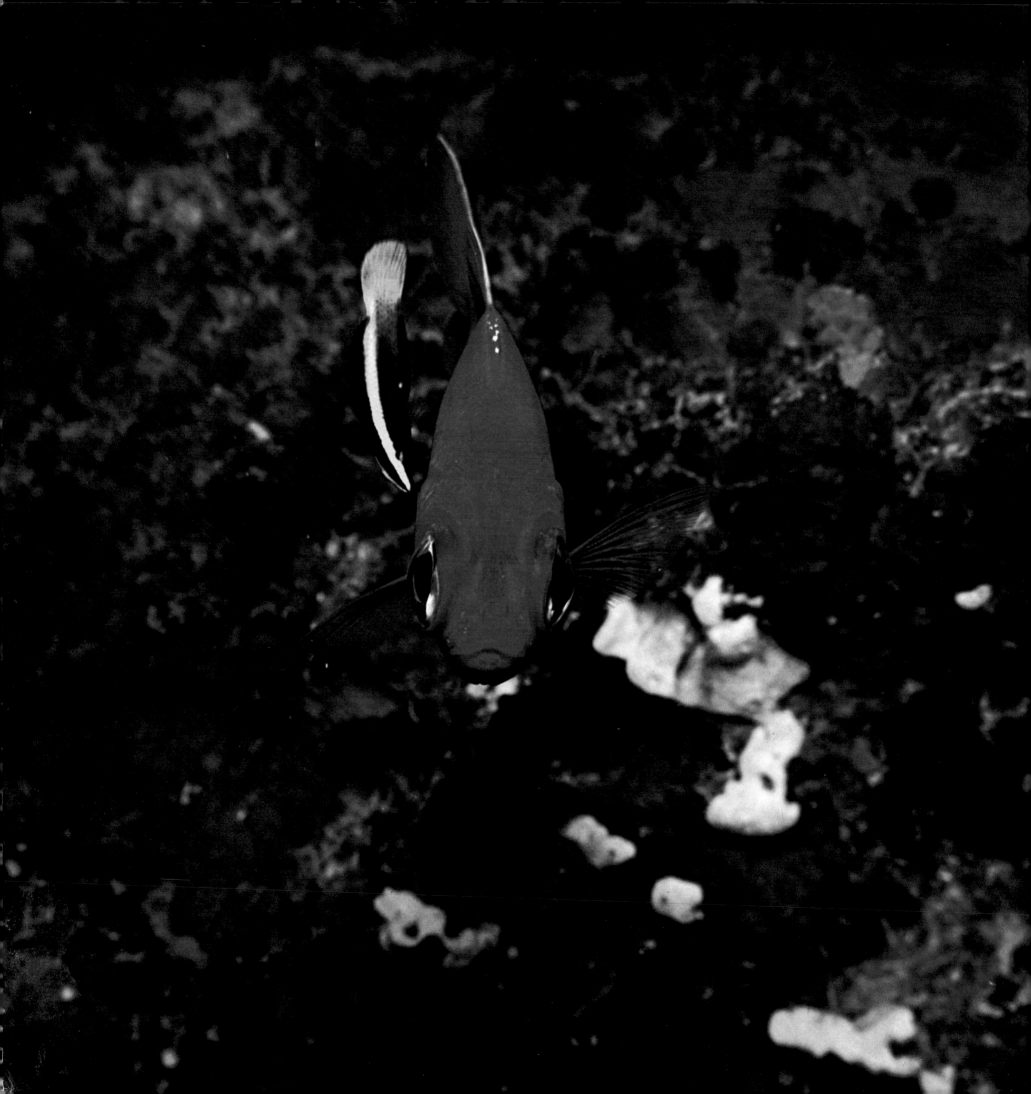

IX

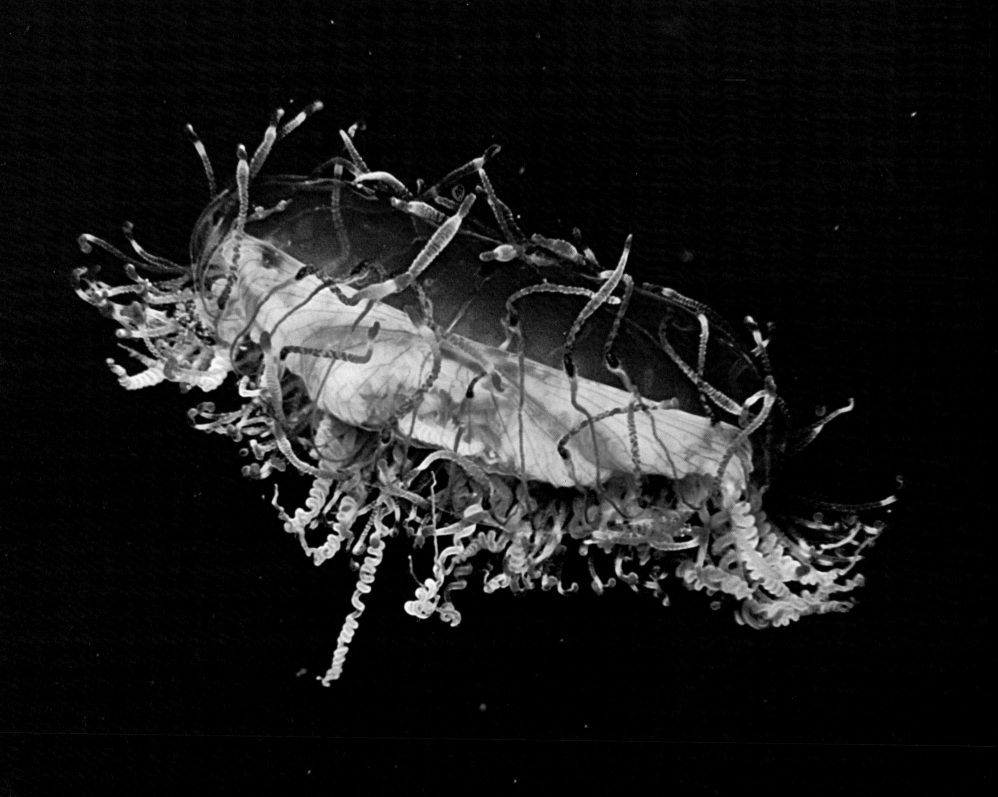

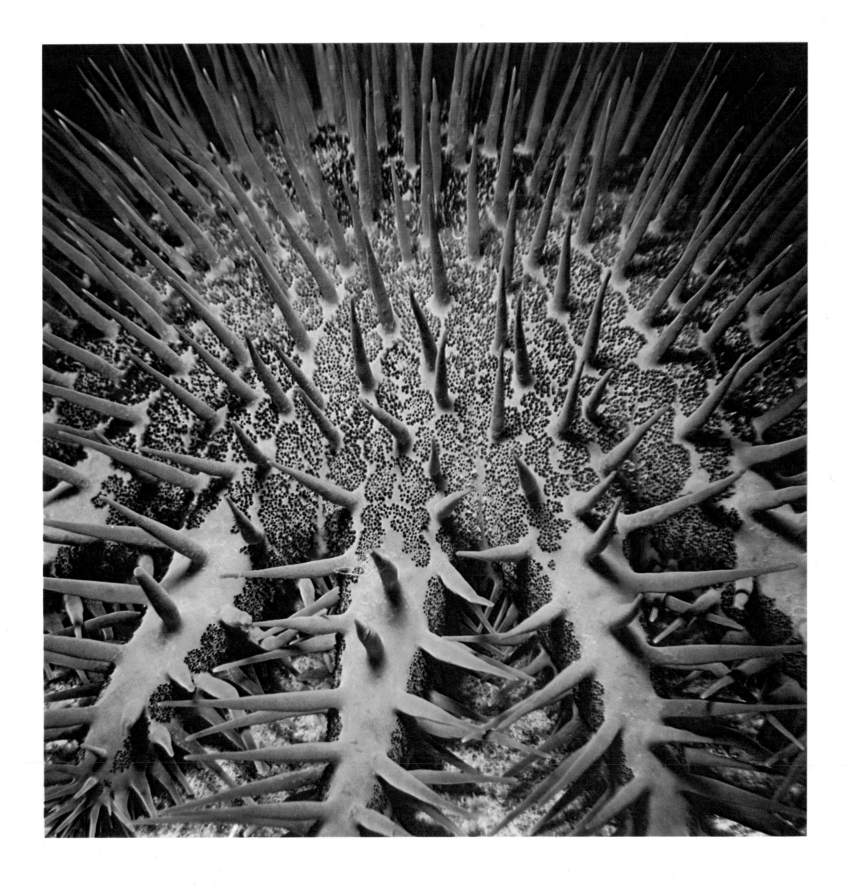

O sweet spontaneous
earth how often have
the
doting

    fingers of
prurient philosophers pinched
and
poked

thee
, has the naughty thumb
of science prodded
thy

   beauty   . how
often have religions taken
thee upon their scraggy knees
squeezing and

buffeting thee that thou mightest conceive
gods
      (but
true

to the incomparable
couch of death thy
rhythmic
lover

    thou answerest

them only with

       spring)

          e.e. cummings

COMMENTARY

These commentaries are designed to give a more complete background of information than would normally be included in captions. With the scientific data and commentaries separated from the photographs, the lovely sea creatures can be appreciated for themselves, uncluttered with words. However, human nature is such that everything must have a name and, it is hoped, an explanation.

The data begin with the common name of each plant and animal, followed by each scientific name (when known), the approximate size of the subjects, the location and estimated depth, the day, month, and year the photograph was made.

One might imagine that such facts give us a firm grasp on our world, but if we stop to think, we realize that common and scientific names, as well as locations, depths, and dates, are human inventions. The universe and all its inhabitants are constantly changing. We try to grasp a fish with the fingers of our thoughts, but the fish, as a continually evolving organism, wriggles out of our grasp. We can feel its movement, but we cannot command it to remain constant for the sake of our science.

We should be aware of the possibility that science has been with us in some form of awareness for as long as we have existed. Many "primitive" peoples know more about animal behavior than do animal behaviorists. Their observations are not invalidated because the spirits of their relatives inhabited animals or the spirits of animals inhabited them. Their thoughts gave meaning to their lives. Scientific man is on a new highway, but the road leads back to a path not greatly behind us in distance or time.

There is nothing thought or created by men and women that is not autobiographical in the fullest sense, having arisen out of our past. All my photographs are autobiographical, as is the film, flashbulbs, and camera. All these things, including my perceptions and my tastes, are a reflection of our culture as they are equally an enrichment of it. These many inventions have grown out of and colored our lives. Scientists may choose to argue all the fine points, but I prefer to remain always a little ignorant of some facts, for I know that man, like every other "species" on this planet, invents himself. Life dreams in many directions, despite all the limitations of existence.

The commentaries which follow may sometimes appear to be irreverent toward "facts," and may indeed poke fun at science a little. A friend of mine once told me that "Life is too serious to take seriously." It is in this spirit that I have written the commentaries. For when one travels in the world, goes over the horizon, so to speak, and comes full circle, there are still more horizons, more than were crossed. When the wanderer returns, no place and every place is home. It is from this newest home that I have written these commentaries, as letters to my children at home.

—Douglas Faulkner
April 1976

1. **Fairy Butterflyfish** *Chaetodon trifasciatus* Mungo Park ● Staghorn Coral *Acropora* sp. ● Raspberry Coral *Pocillopora hemprichii* (Ehrenberg) ● Freckled Blenny *Paracirrhites forsteri* (Bloch & Schneider) ● 1/2 life size ● The Creek, Red Sea, Obhur Kuraa, Saudi Arabia ● 11 meters ● 7 March 1965

In the movie *2001, A Space Odyssey*, the one surviving astronaut finally arrives at a new planet. He descends into a surrealistic world, and as we watch, his spaceship skims low over metallic waves of intense colors. Stanley Kubrick filmed the waters of the earth as his backdrop, then solarized the film and altered the color of the natural scene to evoke an "other world" experience.

Our ocean, at its surface, is a world with which we are familiar. But to a traveler from outer space, all aspects of our planet would seem marvelous and surreal. Here, too, are chromatic waves with their own color and beneath them another planet, populated with living forms which need no movie producer's genius to improve their strangeness or beauty.

2. **Orange-face Butterflyfish** *Chaetodon larvatus* (Ehrenberg) ● Raspberry Coral *Pocillopora hemprichii* (Ehrenberg) ● 3/4 life size ● The Creek, Red Sea, Obhor Kuraa, Saudi Arabia ● 11 meters ● 16 March 1965

Butterflyfishes, like their namesakes, are brightly colored and elegantly patterned. They number more than two hundred species and are conspicuous members of coral reefs. By far the greatest number of butterflyfishes inhabit the tropical Indo-Pacific region, which includes the Red Sea. The Atlantic region has only a half dozen of the total species population. The Indo-Pacific is far older than the Atlantic, and butterflyfishes probably had their genesis there. Those few which inhabit the Caribbean may have migrated to it when the isthmus between North and South America was submerged. Those that survived in isolation from the larger Pacific community evolved to become what they are today. The same is true with corals and other groups of animals, for Atlantic representatives are not as abundant as those of the Pacific. The Indo-

Pacific, of course, is a much vaster region, and its isolated islands provide ideal environments for considerable divergence.

4. **Capricorn Fusiliers** *Pterocaesio capricornis* Smith ● 1/6 life size ● Nature Reserve, Gulf of Aqaba, Eilat, Israel ● 6 meters ● 30 March 1965

Generally, butterflyfishes swim singly or in pairs, nibbling on plants and tiny animals within the confines of their territory. At least one species of butterflyfish congregates to feed on passing plankton. Fusiliers also feed on plankton, but of necessity their swimming behavior is more structured or cohesive. They school because they range a little farther along and out from the reef face.

6. **Hawksbill Turtle** *Eremtmochelys imbricata* (Linnaeus) ● Staghorn Coral *Acropora formosa* (Dana)? ● 1/3 life size ● Ngerumekaol pass, Ulong island, Belau ● 2 meters ● 17 October 1967

Many of the sea's inhabitants, such as staghorn corals, live continually under water breathing dissolved air. Animals like the Hawksbill turtle return to the surface to breathe. Other seagoing reptiles, such as iguanas and sea snakes, also breathe at the surface, as do warm–blooded mammals—the whales and sea lions.

7. **Slinky Ascidians** *Pyrosoma atlanticum* ● 1/4 life size ● Cape Roussin reef, Mare, Loyalty Islands ● 1-1/2 meters ● 26 August 1965

This pyrosoma is a colony of floating ascidians. Each individual animal is seen as a tiny bead of light. Like spun gossamer the colony drifts in the sunlit current, a plankton community feeding on plankton.

8. **Eyed Ctenophore** ● Life size ● Southeast Reef, Long Cay, Glover Reef, Belize ● 1 meter ● 18 January 1973

Among the animals classified as plankton are the ctenophores, of which there are a total of eighty known species. They live in all the oceans of the world and, like the pyrosoma, feed on plankton. Ctenophores are more mobile than the smaller drifting organisms. They evolved from a jellyfish ancestor and are commonly called comb jellies. Ctenophores move through the sea by beating the cilia attached to eight rows of comb plates. Like many plankton, ctenophores are bioluminescent, a state dependent on the nervous stimulation of specialized cells in the animal's light-producing organs. Luciferin and the enzyme protein luciferase are the principal light-generating elements. When ATP, an organic energy carrier, is added to luciferin and in turn luciferase is added in the presence of ions and oxygen, the mixture emits light. Oxygen is burned in the process but with such efficiency that little heat is generated.

At night the sea is a galaxy of little lights. At the Galápagos Islands I once watched sea lions cavort around the "Golden Cachalot." From the crow's nest I could see them below, torpedoing through the darkened waters, clothed in silvery halos of living light.

9. **Galápagos Sea Lion** *Zalophus californianus wollenbackii* ● Approximate length 2 meters ● Gordon Rock, Galápagos Islands, Ecuador ● 1-1/2 meters ● 30 April 1973

Sea lions are creatures between worlds. They are mammals that live much of their lives on land but are making a slow evolutionary return to the sea. On land they move ponderously, and a big bull is a little outlandish as he hobbles up the beach, his large body supported by appendages now evolved more for swimming than walking. In the water sea lions propel themselves with incredible grace and speed. An underwater observer cannot help but notice that most often these creatures swim for the sheer joy of swimming. They play with one another, nipping like puppies, ambushing each other like kittens, executing somersaults and figure eights, propelling themselves up through the surface in a riot of air bubbles and fun.

10. **Dwarf Herring** *Jenkinsia lamprotaenia* (Gosse) ● Life size ● Benwood Wreck, Key Largo, Florida, U.S.A. ● 10 meters ● 11 November 1972

Fusiliers school along the face of a reef, moving back and forth in a limited area, for they sleep on the bottom under coral heads each night. Fishes like the barred jacks swim greater distances while other species that school, such as the dwarf herring, hardly migrate. Pictured here, they inhabit a small cave formed from part of the hull of a sunken ship. These tiny fish always congregate in groups of thousands. When alarmed, they crisscross back and forth, presenting a confusing target to any predator.

11. **Barred Jacks** *Caranx emburyi* (Whitley) ● 1/4 life size ● Cyclone Point reef, Heron Island, Queensland, Australia ● 6 meters ● 11 October 1965

When not alarmed, a school of jacks will swim in uniform formation, but when alerted to danger they change to a crisscrossed pattern of swimming, encircling the predator to confuse it. Many a spear fisherman knows just how difficult it is to concentrate on one fish when many others are simultaneously zooming in from opposite directions.

12. **Cowfish** *Lactoria fornasini* (Bianconi) ● 3/4 life size ● Tanabe Bay, Shirahama, Wakayama-ken, Japan ● 10 meters ● 7 June 1966

Cowfishes are relatively slow swimmers, their bodies not being designed for speed. Their external skeleton, which gives them a measure of protection from predators, equally prohibits them from undulating their bodies like streamlined fishes. However, when alarmed, a cowfish can swim quite rapidly with the help of its pectoral and caudal fins.

The cowfish is named after the horns which project over its eyes. The adults' horns are more stubby than those of the juveniles. With increased size the animal has less need of them. The bony exoskeleton is an unpleasant mouthful for a larger fish. In juveniles the longer horns function like rose thorns. Since many fishes swallow their prey head first, the horns are properly positioned to give a predator a sore throat.

61. Fusiliers *Caesio* sp. ● Approximate length 20 centimeters ● Southwest wall, Cheleu island, Ngemelis islands, Belau ● 21 meters ● 29 July 1973

Jacques-Yves Cousteau believes our planet should be called "Ocean," not "Earth," for indeed the ocean dominates its surface; 70 percent is covered with water. Man came from the sea and, like many another animal, is not content to remain landbound. No doubt our ancestors rarely lived very far from its shores.

63. Crown-of-thorns Sea Star *Acanthaster planci* (Linnaeus) ● Staghorn Coral *Acropora* sp. ● Life size ● Amédée Island reef, New Caledonia ● 5 meters ● 9 September 1965

Looking like an exquisite sunburst, this sea star is traversing a colony of staghorn coral. Its beauty masks a double menace for the spines are venomous, producing painful puncture wounds if touched. Many Indo-Pacific reefs have suffered population explosions of this animal, at which times the sea stars are a plague on the reef, devouring the flesh off corals as they move in a line across the submarine terrain.

Crown-of-thorns most often feed on staghorn corals. Under normal conditions they graze randomly, thereby not entirely destroying any single coral colony. Like other sea stars, they are primarily nocturnal, though they do emerge to feed on rainy days when the sky is heavily overcast. However, when a reef is under stress (often due to man's interference) the crown-of-thorns will be seen feeding on the corals in broad daylight. At such times the sea star must also be under stress, since it prefers darkness to sunlight. As with many humans, population pressures drive it to eat constantly.

64. Sea Star *Asterias vulgaris* Verrill ● Green Sea Urchins *Strongylocentrotus droebachiensis* (Müller) ● Plumose Anemones *Metridium senile* (Linnaeus) ● Brown Mussels *Modiolus modiolus* (Linnaeus) ● Finger Sponge ● 2/3 life size ● Hodgkins Cove, Cape Ann, Massachusetts, U.S.A. ● 3 meters ● 28 August 1967

When I made this photograph, I recorded, by chance, not merely a pleasing visual pattern but a pattern of life. The animals on the piling are spaced out and an amazing variety of living things comprises the community. It is a rich community, but of necessity it is not overcrowded. Since most of the anemones are contracted, it is easy to see the spacing between them. When the tide comes in, they will expand their tentacles, but the tentacles will not greatly overlap and there will be enough plankton for all.

The green urchins are also dispersed, each perhaps gleaning algae from the surface of the piling. Even the two varieties of sponges have found a living space for themselves. So have the groups of brown mussels. Yet nothing is static. A sea star is feeding on one of the mussels. After a time, the empty shells of the mussel will fall to the bottom and there will be a vacant space until another animal, perhaps a bit of encroaching sponge or another mussel, settles there.

65. Orange Tube Corals *Dendrophyllia elegans* van der Horst ● Pink Tube Corals *Dendrophyllia gracilis* Milne Edwards & Haime ● 2/3 life size ● The Great Reef, Bailechesengel island, Ngemelis islands, Belau ● 20 meters ● 23 May 1971

The piling at Hodgkins Cove was an artificial addition to the environment. Probably for a time very little marine life settled on it, because the wood was treated to prevent marine animals from boring into it. Nevertheless the sea prevailed, and eventually plants and animals began to colonize the surface. A coral reef is essentially no different. First a volcanic mountain emerges, and in time the sea's children populate it. As the reef gradually expands, animals and plants leave vacancies, which are quickly filled. Complex arrangements evolve with a profusion of differing life forms.

66. Stalked Ascidian *Polycarpa aurata* (Quoy and Gaimard) ● Sea Fan *Melithaea* sp. ● 1-1/3 times life size ● Mouillage d'Amère, New Caledonia ● 23 meters ● 18 September 1965

This brilliantly colored ascidian is a familiar sight on the outer reefs of New Caledonia, where it lives deep enough not to be subjected to too much turbulence from wave action. However, its stalk enables it to bend with the effects of swells that sometimes reach below the surface as far down as 45 meters. The sea fans are also flexible-bodied and bend with water movements.

The ascidian, although related to backboned animals, lives much like a sponge. It has an incurrent and excurrent opening through which seawater is pumped by means of hairlike cilia. In the process organic matter is collected in the gill basket, which, as its name implies, also functions as a respiratory organ.

67. Feather-duster Worm *Sabellastarte indica* (Savigny) ● Orange Tree Corals *Dendronephthya* sp. ● 1-1/3 times life size ● Tanabe Bay, Shirahama, Wakayama-ken, Japan ● 10 meters ● 16 June 1966

While the ascidian wears its air-gathering gills on the inside of its body, the feather-duster worms are exposed to open water. The worm lacks the pumping mechanism of the ascidian; only the flow of water past its feathery gills nourishes them. The tube worm saves energy by not having to pump water for a living, but in the process its gills are vulnerable to the appetites of passing fishes, such as blennies. In response, tube worms are extremely sensitive to slight displacements of water and to shadows. At such times a tube worm disappears with lightning speed into its protective tube. If no further disturbance occurs, the worm's gills slowly spiral outward and then unfold in a circle of beauty against a backdrop of soft corals.

68. American Goosefish *Lophius americanus* Valenciennes ● 3/4 life size ● Hodgkins Cove, Cape Ann, Massachusetts, U.S.A. ● 6 meters ● 29 August 1967

Like some deep-sea fishes the goosefish has the appearance of being "all mouth." This strange beast is related to the anglerfishes, for it has two dorsal fins serving as a fishing pole with wormlike bait attached. The bait is dangled forward of the mouth, and when almost any size fish is tempted within swallowing distance, the goosefish's Cheshire cat grin suddenly becomes a huge one-way tunnel leading to the stomach. While digestion is in progress, the meter-long goosefish lounges on the sandy bottom, waiting with glazed, iridescent eyes and "gently smiling jaws."

69. Shorthorn Sculpin *Myoxocephalus scorpius* (Linnaeus) ● Life size ● Hodgkins Cove, Cape Ann, Massachusetts, U.S.A. ● 6 meters ● 28 August 1967

Science frowns upon anthropomorphic interpretations on the part of its investigators, but the artist is licensed to be subjective, to be interpretive in the execution of his art. If a fish seems somehow human to him (and he is true to his vision), he conveys his experience. There is more life in an interpretive photograph than in one taken of a dead fish spread out to show the fins and scales. Were I to photograph a fish scale, I would show its beautiful translucence through the play of light on its graceful structure, dynamically ringed as the seasons of a tree are ringed. Only then might it approximate life.

70. Opal Sweepers *Parapriacanthus ransonneti* Steindachner ● 1-1/3 times life size ● Ngerumekaol pass reef, Ulong island, Belau ● 5 meters ● 17 October 1967

Like the dwarf herring, these opal sweepers live much of their lives under a ledge or in a cave beneath a coral formation. As members of a school they seem to function like a single organism. The fish maintain a definite space between one another, and leaders are interchangeable, depending on circumstances. An attack upon one member triggers a response from the entire group. There is no guaranteed safety for the individual in a crowd, however, since lizardfishes feed on sweepers and cardinalfishes, but these communities survive because they reproduce themselves with equal speed. One of the plus marks for schooling is the fact that members are always in close proximity to one another. This aids reproduction.

71. Death Mask Scorpionfish *Inimicus didactylus* (Pallas) ● Life size ● Vata Bay, New Caledonia ● 2 meters ● 12 September 1965

Like other members of the scorpionfish family, this handsome brute can survive as a solitary individual. Its erected dorsal spines are supplemented by venom glands. An unfortunate predator, attempting to swallow this scorpionfish, would put pressure on the spines, which would inject the venom into the predator's flesh. The poison would make the predator's mouth throb, and it would suffer a painful death.

72. Scorpionfish *Scorpaenopsis gibbosa* (Bloch & Schneider) ● 3/4 life size ● Tanabe Bay, Shirahama, Wakayama-ken, Japan ● 11 meters ● 8 June 1966

Scorpionfish are bottom dwellers and swim only reluctantly when disturbed, like the Death Mask from New Caledonia. In every way they resemble the bottom upon which they live, accomplishing this feat by means of shape, leafy appendages, and variegated coloration, and by letting their meals swim to them instead of their going out to search for them.

73. Lizardfish *Synodus variegatus* (Lacépède) ● 1-1/3 times life size ● Kesebekuu pass reef, Mekeald lagoon, Ngeruktabel island, Belau ● 10 meters ● 24 June 1971

Lizardfish, too, are masters of disguise. They rest on the bottom, which might be sand, a rounded coral promontory, or the skeletal debris of staghorn corals encrusted with algae. Here they sit on their pelvic fins like sleek surface-to-air missiles ready for immediate launch. Their prey are often the smaller schooling fishes which pass overhead. When a target is singled out, the lizardfish tilts its head back slightly and rockets upward almost quicker than the eye can follow. When the prey is caught, the lizardfish immediately returns to the safety of the bottom, even before the victim is completely swallowed, lest she fall prey to some larger prowling creature.

74. Orange Clownfish Family *Amphiprion ocellaris* Cuvier • Sea Anemone *Radianthus ritteri* (Kwietniewski) • 1-1/3 times life size • Arlington reef, Queensland, Australia • 8 meters • 19 October 1965

Most of the time, when different marine animals get together they are better off for the association. There are out-and-out parasites, but many other different species associating together in varying degrees of cooperation attest to the survival value of these arrangements and to the idea of cooperation in general.

Some scientists have a mania for keeping things separate—finding that precise slot for classification purposes—but life is a contrary force that keeps mixing things up. Tiny shrimps and crabs live within clams, no doubt providing cleaning services; algae live in the tissues of corals, helping them to produce food and eliminate wastes; shrimps climb into the mouths of groupers to serve as doctors; clownfishes swim through a field of anemone tentacles, cleaning and combing them with their little white teeth, and later, using the same white teeth to snatch up bits of food and plankton from the anemone.

To aid them in their definitions, behavioral scientists refer to one of the partners as the "host," but who is the host when the relationship is most often reciprocal? Like friends, they host each other.

75. Skunk Clownfish *Amphiprion perideraion* Bleeker • Sea Anemone *Radianthus ritteri* (Kwietniewski) • Life size • Point Lefévre reef, Lifou, Loyalty Islands • 20 meters • 2 September 1965

When one dives in the ocean often enough, many degrees of relationships can be observed. The clownfishes are thoroughly entrenched symbionts with their various anemone species. The skunk clownfish usually lives with the anemone *Radianthus ritteri* and is so at ease that it can nuzzle the coelenterate's mouth, removing partially digested foods or wastes. Within the clownfish family a pecking order serves to protect this source of food. Juveniles are chased away from the anemone's mouth when caught stealing food. The older members of the family take turns disciplining the young.

In contrast to the clownfishes, near relatives such as Dacyllus, and in varying degrees some cardinalfishes and small wrasses, are in the process of gaining a closer relationship with anemones. They hover nearby or dart under the crown of tentacles when danger approaches. No doubt a time will come when they, too, have their pecking orders and will swish through their house of tentacles, being guest and host by turns.

76. Sargassumfish *Histro histro* (Linnaeus) • Sargassum Seaweed *Sargassum* sp. • 3 times life size • Public beach, Delray Beach, Florida, U.S.A. • 1/3 meter • 22 June 1963

Just as scorpionfishes are nearly perfect in their adaptation to the benthic sea world, so too the sargassumfish is wonderfully adapted to its surface world of floating seaweed. Using its fins like hands and feet, it climbs around in the algae like a slow-motion jungle gym artist. The amount of movement is critical, for its world is less tame than a playground. Larger sargassumfishes inhabit the seaweed, and the larger fishes prey on their juniors. In a patch of weed, dispersal usually minimizes aggression. A patch of sargassum weed also has limited food resources in the form of crabs, shrimps, and unappetizing nudibranchs which are also intent on survival. Thus competition is fierce.

77. Giant Kelp *Macrocystis pyrifera* (Linnaeus) • 1-1/3 times life size • Fisherman's Cove, Santa Catalina Island, California, U.S.A. • 12 meters • 1 May 1972

Plants and animals of the sea have often evolved similar means of living in response to their water world. Saltwater is quite heavy and greatly supports any organism living in it. Marine plants need not grow massive trunks to support their weight as do trees. It is sufficient that sargassum weed and the giant kelp need only grow strong, slender stems. Their gas-filled bladders provide the lift needed to suspend them in the inner space of the sea. To lift the weight of a balloon, we use helium, which is less dense than air. Any gas is less dense than water and could be contained in a flotation bladder. The giant kelp fills its gas bladders with carbon monoxide.

Marine algae grow quite rapidly, but the giant kelp leads the plant kingdom, growing at the rate of 60 cm per day, sometimes reaching a length of nearly 60 meters from its holdfast on the rocky bottom to where it ends, floating along the sunlit surface above.

The giant kelp, like sargassum weed, provides a home for other creatures. Hydroids, bryozoans, and white-shelled tube worms settle and grow on its fronds. Sediment also collects there until the life-span of an individual frond is concluded in four or five months.

79. Volcano Sponges *Ircinia* sp. • Brain Sponges *Didiscus* new species • Gorgonians, Bryozoans, Coral • 1-1/3 times life size • White Point outer reef, Hog Island, Bay Islands, Honduras • 20 meters • 2 October 1964

Strong wave action generally limits the diversity of plants and animals that can live in shallow water. The richest zones of life in the tropics are at fifteen- to twenty-five-meter depths. Outer reef drop-offs like the up and down surface of a piling always seem to be the most populated regions, due to their proximity to the currents that bathe their surfaces. A constant supply of planktonic organisms is available for all the filter feeders, such as the sponges, bryozoans, and gorgonians pictured here.

80. Strawberry Sponge *Mycale* new species • Algae, Wire Coral • 1-1/4 times life size • The Wall, Small Hope Bay, Andros Island, Bahamas • 35 meters • 14 July 1965

Although scientists rank sponges low on the ladder of biological complexity, no organism is really simple. Even one cell of an organism is a marvelouly intricate structure. A sponge colony, although it has no heart, liver, lungs, and kidneys as do higher animals, is capable of circulating seawater to its cells, which in turn can respire, be nourished, and their metabolic wastes eliminated. Sponges are, by no stretch of the imagination, simple, but in their economical use of the ocean environment they have a functional simplicity. Most often the simplest animals exist age after age, while their more complex neighbors more easily become the victims of evolutionary hazard.

81. Yellow-mouth Sponge • 2/3 life size • The Wall, Small Hope Bay, Andros Island, Bahamas • 30 meters • 12 July 1965

Sponges may be comparatively modest anatomically, but many of them are by no means modest in their garb. The strawberry sponge and this yellow-mouth sponge are as dazzling in their brilliant colors as any fireworks display, and more durable. The strawberry sponge, however, because of the depth at which it lives, needs a little fireworks from the light of a flash bulb to bring out its red color. Water filters out the red in sunlight, rendering the sponge a more brownish color at 36 meters. In contrast, the chrome yellow color of the yellow-mouth sponge is still visible at 30 meters. A diver can see its hue with no artifical light, since yellow is not filtered out until about 45 meters.

All colors, regardless of depth, are altered by the filtering properties of the water. Colors also change with the time of day or night, with the presence of clouds, phases of the moon, atmospheric conditions, and even the seasons of the universe. I have seen the sea's creatures illuminated in many different ways, and there is a beauty in each.

82. Crimson Encrusting Sponge • Pink Tube Corals *Dendrophyllia gracilis* Milne Edwards & Haime • Orange Tube Corals *Dendrophyllia elegans* van der Horst • 1-1/4 times life size • The Great Reef, Bailechesengel island, Ngemelis islands, Belau • 20 meters • 26 August 1973

Sponges assume a variety of shapes. The environment allows for only so many "skyscrapers" in the form of stony corals, gorgonians, sponges, and other assorted creatures. Consequently some plants and animals, including sponges, encrust the relatively flat surface of the reef face, competing with each other for living space. The crimson encrusting sponges are not inhabited by other encrusting organisms, but some sponges are settled on by zoanthids and bryozoans, creating an even richer mosaic of life.

83. Pink Sponge cf. *Eurospongia lobata* Bergquist • Orange Tree Coral *Dendronephthya* sp. • Red Gorgonian • Life size • Southwest wall, Ngcheangel islands, Belau • 21 meters • 10 September 1971

Some sponges have relatively smooth surfaces, while others grow varieties of bumps, ridges, and pointed protrusions. The differing growth forms not only aid in the structural support of the colony but also reflect environmental conditions.

This sponge grew under a ledge where water circulation was diminished. Perhaps its textured surface enabled it to catch plankton which would collide with and be more easily trapped by the protusions. Here, water and food are sucked into tiny holes. The large, circular holes are the excurrent openings which facilitate the outflow of water and wastes.

84. Cinderella Sponge • 1-1/3 life size • Breu reef, Ngercheu island, Belau • 15 meters • 18 May 1971

This delicate sponge, secreted under ledges, inhabits the outer reefs. No two sponges, even of the same species, have exactly the same shape. Size and shape are a consequence of immediate environment, including neighbors and water conditions. This particular sponge is shaped like a fragile drinking cup.

85. Cheese Sponge • Algae • 3/4 life size • Southeast reef, Long Cay, Glover Reef, Belize • 30 meters • 23 January 1973

While size and shape are variable in a sponge, certain of its features do enable an observer to distinguish it from other species. The cheese sponge is one example. Its distinctive surface and color and the prominent excurrent holes set it apart as a creature with its own identity.

However, scientists are more exacting in their classification of sponges, and such superficial features are not entirely sufficient for "positive identification." A sponge specialist takes a small chunk of sponge, dissolves the flesh and spongy skeleton in acid until only the nonsoluble spicules remain. These glasslike structures are more uniformly alike within a species, and are essential for the classification of many sponges.

As yet the cheese sponge and a number of other sponges have no scientific names, an indication of the backlog of discoveries yet to be classified by the world's few sponge specialists.

86. Chalice Sponge *Callyspongia plicifera* (Lamarck) ● Algae ● 2/3 life size ● White Point outer reef, Hog Island, Bay Islands, Honduras ● 20 meters ● 15 September 1964

A number of marine animals fluoresce under ultraviolet light, and in the twilight depths some emit a soft glow of red, green, yellow, or purple. Normally the brightness of the flash used to make the photograph destroys the effect, especially the red colors, but occasionally a faint hint of the glow remains, as on the surfaces of this sponge.

87. Pottery Sponges *Agelas* new species ● 1-1/4 times life size ● Fresh Creek Channel, Andros Island, Bahamas ● 35 meters ● 15 July 1965

When one glances over the photographs, it is evident that the volcano sponges, strawberry sponges, cheese sponges, udder sponges, as well as these pottery sponges, have reproduced themselves by division—somewhat as a single cell reproduces itself by splitting into two. In these different colonies the animals are in various stages of growth, and their offspring are quite a part of themselves.

88. Egg Yolk Sponges ● Red Encrusting Sponge ● Life size ● The Great Reef, Bailechesengel island, Ngemelis islands, Belau ● 25 meters ● 6 July 1971

When I was young, the school I attended required that I take part in an annual public-speaking contest. I was terrified because I felt I had nothing of interest to say. Since that terror still haunts me, I always begin a lecture by first projecting photographs. After they become the center of attention, I relax enough to speak about them. Nevertheless, at some point during my presentation, I let the colors and forms speak for themselves because I am rendered silent by the beauty before me.

89. Udder Sponges *Leucetta floridana* (Haeckel) ● Wire Sponge ● Life size ● The Wall, Small Hope Bay, Andros Island, Bahamas ● 65 meters ● 13 August 1968

Shallow-water sponges, living on the reef flats at depths of a few meters down to five or six meters, are often rounded and densely constructed. In contrast, many deep-water sponges are quite delicate, with thin walls, or they are greatly elongated and elaborately branched. No waves or strong currents disturb them. At 65 meters much less organic matter is suspended in the water, a fact easily observed because the visibility at that depth is much increased, often exceeding 60 meters horizontally. Seasonal changes do cause upwelling, which is accompanied by plankton blooms as the sea's creatures give birth. But much of the time the deeper waters are less populated by plankton.

As a result, many sponges living there have a sparse diet, particularly those inhabiting the underledges.

90. Phallus Sponge ● Zoanthids ● Red Encrusting Sponge ● 3/4 life size ● The Wall, South Pigeon Cay, Andros Island, Bahamas ● 65 meters ● 20 August 1968

What's in a name? This sponge by any other name would not lose its unmistakable resemblance, though the similarity is confined strictly to its shape. The little wine-colored spots are zoanthids, anemone-like animals which inhabit the surface of many sponges.

When one considers that this sponge filter-feeds, and that its surface is a network of tiny "mouths," one may wonder how the zoanthids manage to colonize the colony without being eaten. The process may very well be a hit-and-miss affair. Some zoanthids fall prey, while others, like adept parachutists, manage to miss the trees and land on the ground. When this happens it is the sponge which gets eaten. The zoanthids, by some process, eat away at the surface of the sponge—equivalent to a clearing of the land for habitation.

In another context, a Chinese proverb gracefully defines such paradoxes: "When the river rises the fish eat the ants; when the river falls the ants eat the fish."

91. Fan Sponge *Phakellia folium* Schmidt ● 1-1/3 times life size ● The Wall, Small Hope Bay, Andros Island, Bahamas ● 73 meters ● 16 August 1968

Although this photograph was made eight years ago, it still seems new to me. For a human long accustomed to walking on land and breathing unlimited air, to dive to 73 meters is a somewhat unsettling experience. At least it was then. I recall that I would never have taken such risks merely to sightsee, as I sometimes do now.

Having crossed that barrier of fear, I would just as confidently go to the moon and beyond to photograph as to 73 meters. In fact, I would rather go to the moon than dive to the *Andrea Doria*, which sleeps silently in 75 meters of North Atlantic water. But the

sea life growing on wrecks interests me. When I think of it, the reef is like a wrecked ship, hull encrusted with life. Its deep sediment-filled corridors are silent now, but on its surface exist strange, beautiful creatures.

93. Crimson Sea Whips *Juncella gemmacea* (Valenciennes) ● 1-1/3 times life size ● Ngerumekaol pass, Ulong island, Belau ● 14 meters ● 8 October 1967

It is unfortunate that the coral photographs in this book cannot be spread out on the floor as I have seen them, to be viewed together. This would allow a much keener awareness of the diversity of corals and their relatives. Since most of the corals are presented in abstract with only a portion of the colony in the photograph, each species contrasts greatly with the others. These crimson sea whips are gorgonians with flexible skeletons. The daisy coral has a rigid skeleton with highly flexible large-bodied polyps. Both species feed on plankton, but their structures are adapted to the requirements of the different environments in which they live.

94. Tree Coral *Dendronephthya* sp. ● Life size ● Mbere reef, New Caledonia ● 20 meters ● 14 September 1965

Corals like the crimson sea whips have skeletons composed of a horny substance known as gorgonian. Others have calcium carbonate (limestone) skeletons. This tree coral is known as a "soft coral" because it has no "skeleton" in the proper sense of the word. Its only claim to a skeleton is the many fibrous spicules embedded in its fleshy trunk and branches. The spicules are not like those found in sponges. Tree coral spicules give the colony structural strength while allowing it to expand and contract in its response to the tides. When the tide is flowing, the coral expands to feed on passing plankton. At slack tide the trunk, branches, and foliage of the colony shrivel up into a prickly mass. Since many small reef fishes feed upon the polyps and flesh of corals, it is advantageous for the coral to gather everything up and store it away until feeding time comes around again.

95. Tom Robbins' Weenie Coral *Euphyllia fimbriata* (Spengler) ● Life size ● Patch reef, Mekeald lagoon, Ngeruktabel island, Belau ● 30 meters ● 6 November 1967

Giving common names to marine animals is sometimes pleasant and sometimes not so pleasant. Scientists, of course, work with their own adopted language initiated by Linnaeus. Occasionally even their system breaks down because generic and specific designations are not capable of pigeonholing plants and animals which are obviously diverging and becoming separate species. As a consequence another category surfaces, like the Galápagos sea lion which is a "sub species" of the California sea lion. As regards corals, some are so variable from one isolated population to another that scientists have nearly given up trying to classify them with names.

If scientists have their problems, so do laymen, informed or not so well-informed. An animal found worldwide has multiple names, not all of them in English. To further complicate matters, some animals, though they may not look alike, do resemble something in common. The mushroom coral, *Fungia*, resembles the underside of a mushroom, and its generic name attests to the fact. Another coral, this *Euphyllia*, also resembles a mushroom, but in this instance a sliced mushroom or a bowl of sliced mushrooms. Presented with this dilemma, I named *Euphyllia* "sausage coral," instead.

After having made my choice and bearing with it for several nagging, dissatisfied years, I became friends with a novelist, Tom Robbins. Robbins, in addition to his love of words, salivates like Pavlov's dog for weenies, hot dogs, and sausages of all sizes, origins, and species. He is equally a mushroom gourmet and forsakes his typewriter each spring and fall to hunt the forests north of Seattle. Thus we have the new revised, enlarged common name: "Tom Robbins' Weenie Coral." On hearing the news, Robbins was delighted, but I am still not entirely satisfied. Perhaps in a few years I'll decide the coral is a subspecies and rename it "Tom Robbins' Mushroom-Weenie Coral." I could revise the name now while I'm thinking about it, since I know the coral will continue to evolve, but, cautious scientist that I am, I'll wait until I have the facts.

96. Gauguin Sea Fan *Melithaea squamata* (Nutting) ● 1-1/3 times life size ● Ngerumekaol pass reef, Ulong island, Belau ● 8 meters ● 8 October 1967

While on the subject of names, let me add that Gauguin, Van Gogh, and Vivaldi have vitally influenced my life and work. In my book *This Living Reef* I was able to pay homage to Van Gogh and Vivaldi. I felt particularly sad that there was no subject in the book to which I could affix Gauguin's name, for his spirit is of the tropics. Gauguin delighted in colors as much as I and he taught me how he saw them, not in isolation, but as part of the fabric of life.

The Gauguin Sea Fan evokes for me the essence of the artist and man. It is dynamically structured as any organism is always structured, but it is *open* and it bends, sways in slow motion as do the golden people who populate his paintings.

97. Orange Tube Corals *Dendrophyllia* sp. ● Life size ● North Wall, Isla Caldwell, Isla Floreana, Galápagos Islands, Ecuador ● 12 meters ● 7 May 1973

The major reef-building corals are restricted to the tropics. Other corals, which live in cold, deep water, do not form typical reefs because they are small in size or grow too gradually to contribute appreciably to the total reef superstructure. Nevertheless all corals do have positive growth effect on the environment. Most of the tube corals do not grow to large sizes, but their presence on a reef face aids in its presentation, since they displace other organisms which attack and break it down—such as boring sea urchins and bivalves which compete for the same living space.

The non-reef-building "ahermitypic" corals populate recessed areas in deeper water where the sunlight is lessened. They are so named because they lack symbiotic algae in their tissues that are essential for the prodigious production of limestone which accompanies rapid, sustained growth.

Reef corals are restricted in their distribution primarily when temperature and sunlight decrease. Tube corals are not so greatly affected. They are more cosmopolitan in their distribution, for they live in the not-so-warm waters of the inland sea of Japan and range as far east as the Galápagos Islands off Ecuador. In Belau, which is entirely tropical, the tube corals range from the outer face of the barrier reef, through the passes, into the more secluded areas of the lagoons where many outreef corals are unable to live. Very often it is these diminutive ocean inhabitants which, like plankton, have much to do with the construction of a reef.

98. Cerianthid Anemone ● Black-striped Cardinalfish *Apogon* sp. ● Shrimps and Algae ● Life size ● Banc Gail, New Caledonia ● 30 meters ● 28 September 1965

Anemones, relatives of corals, are solitary polyps without skeletons. Most anemones are considerably larger than the polyps of most colonial corals. Anemones don't construct limestone skeletons, but some, like the cerianthid from New Caledonia, fashion tubes of hardened slime and sand grains around their bodies for protection. Other species live in a tube hidden in the sand and, in both instances, rapidly retreat into their tubes when disturbed.

The two nearby cardinalfish and the shrimps clinging to the tube of the New Caledonia cerianthid demonstrate the value association between different species. Cerianthid tentacles are surfaced with stinging nematocysts used for trapping plankton and for self-defense. The other animals take advantage of the cerianthid's arsenal, not unlike small countries which rely on their larger cousins. The more complete the relationship the more dependent each is upon the other to satisfy certain needs.

99. Plumose Anemone *Metridium senile* (Linnaeus) ● Brown mussels *Modiolus modiolus* (Linnaeus) ● Green Sea Urchins *Strongylocentrotus drobachiensis* (Müller) ● 2/3 life size ● Hodgkins Cove, Cape Ann, Massachusetts, U.S.A. ● 4 meters ● 28 August 1967

The cerianthid retreats within its protective tube; the plumose anemone contracts like the tree corals when not feeding. Some plumose anemones greatly expand their columns to several feet in height. Therefore they must not be subject to predation, or other factors must aid their survival.

A multitude of tiny hairlike tentacles atop the plumose column are well designed to trap plankton and other animals to satisfy the anemone. Off Vancouver Island I have seen moon jellyfishes collide with plumose and cerianthid anemones. At first a cerianthid anemone holds the pulsating jellyfish with its tentacles, drawing it down to the centrally located mouth. As the jellyfish is consumed, it is rotated like a scoop of ice cream atop a cone, until finally nothing of the neat, translucent ball of flesh remains.

100. Papua Jellyfish *Mastigias papua* (Lesson) ● 1-1/4 times life size ● Jellyfish Marine Lake, Oreor island, Belau ● 1 meter ● 24 August 1969

Jellyfishes, along with corals and sea anemones, are Coelenterates. These watery creatures vary in size from 3 centimeters in diameter up to the giant lion's mane jellyfish *Cyanea capillata* of Arctic waters that sometimes reach 2 or 2-1/2 meters across, with tentacles trailing for 30 meters or more, and a total mass weighing up to a ton.

The Papua jellyfish of tropical Pacific waters is more modest. This one inhabits the interior marine lakes of Belau and its trailing tentacles or "clubs" are atrophied appendages. Members of the same species inhabiting the lagoons have more fully developed clubs which trail several feet behind the bell. These clubs are more equipped with stinging cells for feeding and self-defense.

In the words of one humorist, jellyfishes are little more than organized water: 95 percent water, 4 percent salts, and one percent organic matter. If the Papua jellyfish —the moon jellyfish—is merely organized water, I can only marvel at its geometry!

101. Moon Jellyfish *Aurelia aurita* (Linnaeus) ● 3/4 life size ● Southeast reef, Long Cay, Glover Reef, Belize ● 5 meters ● 19 January 1973

Moon jellyfish encircle the oceans as the moon circles the earth. These animals are probably the most common of the sea's jellyfishes, inhabiting both tropic and arctic regions. The moon jelly is aptly named, for it is rounded like the moon. This photograph even shows the "Man in the Moon." His jolly nose, cheeks, and smiling mouth are formed of the silhouettes of four frilly oral appendages. His irregularly rounded

eyes are formed of two of his four gonads, the upper two forming his quizically arched eyebrows.

The life history of the moon jelly is similar to that of many jellyfishes and shows how sexual reproduction evolved out of asexual reproduction. However, the jellyfishes still have the best of both worlds. In the "adult" jellyfish stage there are males and females, the sexes being differentiated. When reproduction occurs, the zygote develops into a small larva known as the planula which propels itself about in the water by means of its cilia. Although it can swim, it is a plankton because it cannot outswim the currents. But in time it settles on the bottom and is transformed into a hydroidlike creature, the scyphistoma, which grows to 13 centimeters in length. Then it divides asexually by fission into a number of saucerlike animals called ephyra. When they have finally separated, one from another, they leave the bottom as free swimming jellyfishes again. The medusa grow to adulthood and can now reproduce sexually again in an unending life cycle.

102. Pink Tube Corals *Dendrophyllia gracilis* Milne Edwards & Haime ● Lace Ascidians *Didemnum nekozita* Tokioka ● Red, Blue, and Yellow Sponges ● 1-1/3 times life size ● The Great Reef, Bailechesengel island, Ngemelis islands, Belau ● 12 meters ● 26 July 1973

The pink tube corals, lace ascidians, and assorted sponges all feed on plankton. With such an abundance of predators it is a wonder that there is enough food to go around, and even more amazing that any plankton manages to settle and grow on a rock surface richly populated. Fortunately the plankton proliferate. Also it is clear from this and other photographs in the book that some plants and animals merely settle on the surfaces of other plants and animals. Lace ascidians settle and grow on certain sponges and crustose coralline algae. Tube coral larvae settle in tiny bare spots and manage to grow and multiply themselves. If a sponge expands its size and surrounds the skeletal base of a tube coral, the coral still continues to grow and may eventually become an archipelago of islands surrounded by a sea of sponge.

Sponges and ascidians probably feed day and night, while the tube corals in Belau feed primarily at night. Since the expanded tentacles of the tube corals overreach their neighbors when feeding, it is beneficial to the sponges and ascidians that the corals feed mainly at night and not all the time. This photograph, taken during the day, shows the tube corals at rest, their orange-colored tentacles contracted and hidden away within the crown of each tube's chalice.

103. Bouquet Flower Coral *Lobophyllia hemprichii* (Ehrenberg) ● Life size ● Northeast Cove, Ngeruktabel island, Belau ● 11 meters ● 7 July 1973

Scientists once thought that corals feed only at night. This belief was reinforced because they knew that the plankton migrates vertically, ascending at night and descending during the day. Though some corals feed only at night, many others, mainly the gorgonians, sea fans, and soft corals, feed day and night when the tides are flowing. It is the stony corals which feed mainly at night, although a number of staghorn and *Porites* corals feed regularly during the day, while others feed during rainy days when the sky is overcast.

Many corals do feed at night because of an increase in plankton. Also, their delicate polyps would be eaten by many of the reef fishes during the day. Since most of these fishes sleep at night, the corals can feed unmolested at that time. However, it is also possible that much metabolic activity exists within the coral colony during the daylight hours. The colony is not really inactive merely because its polyps are contracted. The flesh of many reef corals contain symbiotic algae which need sunlight, for photosynthesis is an essential part of some corals' metabolism. Undoubtedly, corals do most of their growing when their polyps are contracted, because the sunlight is better able to reach the algae, thus increasing the entire metabolic process.

In my still limited experience of the sea I have discovered that there is always a multiplicity of reasons that marine organisms behave the way they do.

104. Castle Coral *Pachyseris rugosa* (Lamarck) ● 3/4 life size ● Northeast Cove, Ngeruktabel island, Belau ● 10 meters ● 14 July 1973

The castle coral feeds at night. During the day its tiny polyps are contracted and a sparse layer of flesh barely conceals the colony's underlying structure. The growth ridges of the coral are seen stacked one upon another.

In contrast, the Bouquet Flower Coral skeleton is greatly concealed by the animal's flesh, even though the feeding tentacles are not expanded. The general configuration of the skeleton can be seen, but it is difficult to imagine that this coral's hidden skeleton is armed with jagged, razor-edged ridges. I once bumped my knee against it and learned unforgettably.

Such skeletal structures definitely encourage would-be predators to look elsewhere for a meal. Corals not so endowed, such as the staghorn and *Porites* corals, are more easily preyed upon. I don't recall ever seeing any fish or sea star prey upon the castle coral, possibly because the colony is more skeleton than flesh.

105. Daisy Coral *Alveopora allingi* Höffmeister • 1-1/3 times life size • Kesebekuu pass reef, Mekeald lagoon, Ngeruktabel island, Belau • 14 meters • 26 October 1967

The daisy coral is one stony coral that feeds during the day. Since it lives in the lagoons and since crocodiles feed in Belau's lagoons at night, I have not been tempted to discover if the daisy corals also feed at night.

In contrast to many other stony corals, the flowerlike polyps of the daisy coral are much enlarged. Inasmuch as the daisy coral's polyps are nearly always expanded during the day, and most of the colony's flesh is in the polyps, much of the growth processes of this species probably occurs when the polyps are expanded and feeding. Symbiotic algae give to this and to other corals much of their color. Often I have seen this coral with pure white polyps on a part of the colony. The white polyps seem to be devoid of their algae. Evidently, at certain times the algae vacate or are evacuated from the polyps.

106. Stinging Bubble Coral *Physogyra lichtensteini* (Milne Edwards & Haime) • 1-1/4 times life size • Kesebekuu pass reef, Mekeald lagoon, Ngeruktabel island, Belau • 10 meters • 5 November 1967

Although corals have stinging nematocysts for protection and to immobilize prey, not all nematocysts are powerful enough to irritate human skin seriously. Divers discover that some corals merely scratch, but those that do sting deserve much respect.

The stinging bubble coral skeleton, unlike other stony corals, is quite fragile, filled with numerous open spaces. If a parrotfish were to graze this colony, considerable damage would occur to the skeleton. The colony's more powerful nematocysts protect it from parrotfish gourmets.

We will probably never know which came first—the colony's nematocysts or its fragile skelton—but the nematocysts make possible the fragile skeleton. This coral colony could have developed powerful nematocysts in response to attacks upon it, just as other corals responded by constructing jaw-breaking or lip-splitting skeletons.

107. Tree Corals *Dendronephthya* sp. • Life size • The Creek, Red Sea, Obhor Kuraa, Saudi Arabia • 12 meters • 9 March 1965

Some of my friends have decided that this coral looks less like a tree and more like someone's lungs. I agree. It also reminds me of arteries and veins. Many more associations are also valid, because trees, lungs, and circulatory systems, like rivers, function similarly and are similar in appearance. Their streams and tributaries are the thoroughfares for the elements of life, returning and departing.

108. Orange Tube Corals *Dendrophyllia arbuscula* van der Horst • 1-1/4 times life size • Tanabe Bay, Shirahama, Wakayama-ken, Japan • 15 meters • 19 June 1966

While the tube corals in tropical regions feed primarily at night, those inhabiting cooler regions, such as Japanese and Galápagos waters, feed during the day. This is true of many of the colder water forms of life. In the tropics crabs and sea stars are mostly nocturnal, but in colder waters these invertebrates are active during the day.

There is greater diversity of marine life on a coral reef than in colder seas, but those plants and animals that have managed to survive in cold water are quite abundant. Competition is probably just as great and in fact is greatest between members of the same species. Therefore, cold water crabs, urchins, mollusks, and others, unlike many of their nocturnal relatives in the tropics, waste not the day.

109. Siphonogorgia Coral *Siphonogorgia* sp. • 1-1/3 times life size • Reunion reef, Faulkner Island, Belau • 8 meters • 17 August 1969

In early 1976 a typhoon passed within several hundred miles of Belau. It was not a full-force typhoon, but the winds were out of the southwest. Prior to the storm I happened to be diving in several locations around Belau, all with southwest exposure, for at that season those particular areas are relatively sheltered reefs. Not so during the storm. Great swells crashed upon the reefs and destroyed many corals.

When the storm finally abated after five windy days, I returned to the reefs to continue my work. Familiar corals, once growing along the edge of the reef, were now missing. One *Porites* coral head dislodged from the fore reef tumbled down the cliff face, collided with another coral fifteen meters down, and they both met an uncertain fate far below.

Some staghorn corals grow their stony structures like platters raised upon pedestal-like bases. In a sense they have adopted the spread-out shape of the sea fans, though, unlike them, their flat surface is oriented horizontally to catch the sunlight for photosynthesis.

Thirty meters beneath the surface, I encountered the sad wreckage of a once beautiful platter staghorn coral, resting precariously on a small ledge. Despite its poor condition, I immediately recognized it. I swam the thirty meters to the surface, and my suspicion was confirmed. The platter coral no longer adorned its usual place on the reef. Only a bare patch of limestone remained.

Days later I dived on another, normally sheltered reef and, to my dismay, found many platter corals overturned, their pedestal bases pointing skyward. Fortunately such storms are not common and platter corals are widely distributed vertically and regionally. Thus many always survive, though their structure has its flaws.

Gorgonians and sea fans, which also have flattish surfaces but are oriented vertically and can bend under such stress, weather such storms easily, though they have a few structural problems directly related to the human predator. Unlike the platter corals, sea fans are light and, initially, brighly colored. Thus, the trophy hunters break them off and take them home to hang on their walls. When dry, sea fans and gorgonians fade and become brittle. Their delicate branches break off, and they are lovely no more.

111. Chambered Nautilus *Nautilus macromphalus* Sowerby • 3/4 life size • Mbere reef, New Caledonia • 30 meters • 26 September 1965

Several hundred million years ago, when the ocean covered much of what is now North America, the nautiloids were in their golden age. Giants, with nine- and fourteen-foot shells, propelled themselves through the depths. In all there were over 2500 species grouped among 300 genera. Today there is but one genus, *Nautilus*, which dates back some 180 million years. The Nautilus is so well adapted to its particular world that its basic shell structure, at least, has changed very little during that great span of time.

The nautiloids actually date back to the Precambrian period some 600 million years ago, but the earliest representatives had straight shells. In time the shells became coiled and their utility proved itself.

The nautiluses, along with cuttlefishes, squids, and octopuses, belong to the group of mollusks known as cephalopods, which means "head-footed." Such an idea is awkward for the human to comprehend, considering that our heads and feet are at opposite ends of our bodies. The cephalopods seem not to be bothered, however, for they don't really have feet. They have tentacles and arms which encircle their mouths in a most convenient location to catch food, hold, and eat it with minimum effort. These same appendages are also used for self-defense, moving about, and for courtship embrace. Obviously, having their brains near their toes does not inhibit cephalopods.

112. Rooster-comb Oyster *Lopha cristagalli* (Linnaeus) • Yellow Tube Corals *Tubastraea coccinea* Lesson • Encrusting Sponge • Life size • Bedulyaus point reef, Teongel pass, Ngerchol island, Belau • 11 meters • 7 June 1970

These rooster-comb oysters, encrusted with sponge and tube corals, differ greatly from the chambered nautilus. The oysters are attached to the under ledge of a large coral formation, and only their young are mobile as plankton, swimming in the currents.

Mollusks are divided into five major classes, the bivalves being one. They include clams and mussels. In all five classes there are more than 80,000 species, so it is not difficult to understand why the rooster-comb oyster looks totally unlike a nautilus, a nudibranch, or cowrie.

Like the encrusting sponges and the tube corals, the oysters are plankton feeders, and all these animals are situated so that the tides bathe them.

113. Chambered Nautilus *Nautilus macromphalus* Sowerby • 2/3 life size • Mbere reef, New Caledonia • 21 meters • 26 September 1965

Octopuses have eight arms. Squids and cuttlefishes have ten, two of which are longer, extendable tentacles used for grasping prey at greater distances. The nautilus has more tentacles than all its relatives combined. The tentacles are sheathlike, housing feelerlike appendages called cirri. Each cirrus can be extended outward or withdrawn into each tentacle. Nautiluses, unlike their relatives, do not have suckers. The cirri have adhesive ridges which adhere to objects such as a reef wall when the nautilus wants to rest. At first the nautilus grasps the wall and then pulls itself toward it until the cirri are retracted. When the nautilus is firmly up against the wall, the back of its protective shell faces outward to the open water. The disruptive markings on the shell also aid the animals, for they help to conceal its presence from would-be predators.

114. Cuttlefish *Solitosepia liliana* Irdale • Staghorn Coral *Acropora* sp. • 1/3 life size • Amédée Island reef, New Caledonia • 2 meters • 9 September 1965

In the spring of the year, which is September in the southern hemisphere, the cuttlefishes come into shallow water around the reefs of New Caledonia to mate and lay their eggs. One spring day I was swimming on the reef of Amédée Island and came across a lovely female cuttlefish hovering above the coral. I cautiously approached to photograph her. Presently a male glided up to her and began flashing neon blue colors over his body in waves. He approached still closer and spread his arms wide. With his two top arms he stroked the female's forehead until she spread her arms to receive him. Within a few moments they locked in an embrace. Thus joined, they glided gracefully over the reef, making me think of lovers floating over the rooftops in a Chagall painting. Anthropomorphic or not, my impression was of something definitely tender. After several minutes they parted and went their separate ways. Later the female would deposit her fertilized eggs in a mass on the ceiling under a nearby coral ledge and leave them to their fate.

115. Cuttlefish *Solitosepia liliana* Irdale ● Staghorn Coral *Acropora* sp. ● 1-1/2 times life size ● Amédée Island reef, New Caledonia ● 3 meters ● 9 September 1965

The nautilus is the only cephalopod that cannot change its body color. Since it is primarily nocturnal and lives in deep water where the light level is low, even during the day, subtle color changes are probably not necessary to its survival. Not so with the octopus, squid, and cuttlefish. These animals change their body colors very rapidly to approximate the colors of their surroundings. They also show their moods, just as humans blush when embarrassed or flush when angry. The cuttlefish accomplishes these quick-change feats by the use of chromatophores in its flesh, that are expanded and contracted to produce various patterns of colors. It is not surprising that these animals, which, like fishes, have sophisticated eyes for keener vision, have—also like fishes—evolved chromatophores and the subtle use of them for protection against visual hunters. These soft-bodied cephalopods are masters of disguise with their impressionistic use of colors, accomplishing change in an instant.

116. Spanish Dancer Nudibranch *Hexabranchus imperialis* Kent● Life size ● Doking Point reef, Lifou, Loyalty Islands ● 8 meters ● 31 August 1965

Nudibranchs are gastropod mollusks that have dispensed with their shells, perhaps for greater mobility and ease of movement. As a defense their flesh tastes unpleasant to predators. They advertise the fact with their conspicuous body colors just as the venomous lionfishes are elaborately colored and patterned to warn predators.

Nudibranchs are so called because their gills are exposed to the water. Most nudibranchs, like their shelled relatives, crawl over the bottom, feeding on algae and other organisms, such as sponges. One nudibranch, at least, consumes a sponge little by little over a period of weeks. Like a wrecking crew, the nudibranch doesn't stop until the building is demolished.

The Spanish Dancer not only crawls on the bottom, but, as its name implies, also takes flight by undulating the fleshy ridges of its body like the Spanish dancer who undulates the hem of the skirt held in her hands.

Some nudibranchs as well as flat worms have decided that a totally benthic existence is not for them. Some reptiles did the same thing when they leaped into the air on their way to becoming birds.

117. Alabaster Nudibranchs *Dirona albolineata* (Bergh) ● Devil's Apron Algae ● 1-1/2 times life size ● West Point, Brandon Island, Departure Bay, Vancouver Island, B.C., Canada ● 11 meters ● 12 November 1969

The many flame-shaped gills of these nudibranchs are easily seen here, as their internal structure is revealed through transparent flesh. Nudibranchs are quite common in the tropics, but the colder, subarctic regions seem to spill them forth upon the shallow coastal regions like a burst piñata—toys of many colors, all the lovelier when contrasted with this devil's apron alga leaf, flecked with other snowy organisms.

118. Chambered Nautilus *Nautilus pompilius* Linnaeus ● 3/4 life size ● The Great Reef, Bailechesengel island, Ngemelis islands, Belau; trapped at 125 meters, photographed at 30 meters ● 24 March 1975

There are three species of chambered nautilus. *Nautilus macromphalus* lives in New Caledonia and the Loyalty Islands. *Nautilus scrobiculatus* lives in the Solomon Islands and the New Hebrides. *Nautilus pompilius* is the most widespread of the group, ranging from Fiji, west to the Philippines and many areas in between, including New Guinea, Australia, and Belau. In Australia and Belau the animal is much larger than those living in Philippine waters.

Here, the male (foreground) clings to the female's shell while she swims in the depths. Males and females can be distinguished, one from another, by the size and shape of the shell. The male's shell is usually larger, and the last chamber (occupied by the animal) is wider to accommodate the extra space required by the male's large spadix, its secondary sex organ. The female does not have a spadix, and her shell opening is narrower. Obviously, in this side view of the pair, sex differences are not apparent. Also, females cling to males and males cling to other males, so proximity is no indication of sex.

119. Chambered Nautilus *Nautilus pompilius* Linnaeus ● 1/2 life size ● The Great Reef, Bailechesengel island, Ngemelis islands, Belau ● trapped at 125 meters, photographed at 30 meters ● 13 March 1975

The nautiluses, like squids and cuttlefishes, have a siphon or, as it is called in the nautilus, the hyponome. Octopuses, squids, and cuttlefishes have a closed jet tube through which water is forced for propulsion. In the nautilus the hyponome is not closed, and the two ventral flaps usually overlap. The nautilus is not designed for speed, because it lives around rocky areas near the bottom or in caves where rapid

propulsion is not essential. Nevertheless it does need to move, and the hyponome is its primary propulsion system. The hyponome is quite flexible and can be directed straight ahead, to either side, upward, downward, or even down and backward under the lower edge of the shell to propel the nautilus "forward" (as seen in this photograph). When the nautilus moves "forward"—as we think of it—the animal extends its cirri. They function like cats' whiskers for feeling their surroundings. Some cirri also function as chemo-receptors, that "smell" the food. When food is located, the cirri grasp and draw it to the nautilus's parrotlike beak to be eaten.

120. Octopus *Octopus* sp. ● Crustose Coralline Algae ● 1/2 life size ● Daphne Island, Galápagos Islands, Ecuador ● 12 meters ● 29 April 1973

The octopus is probably the artist supreme of cephalopod ingenuity when it comes to matching its surroundings. Since it ranges the bottom, it must match its ever-changing backdrop as quickly as it moves across it. When it is resting in one spot, it even shapes its body to become a part of the terrain, bumps, colors, and all.

Octopuses are generally nocturnal, especially in tropic waters. Usually they live in burrows dug from the sand and coral rocks. A diver can usually spot an octopus home by the garbage dump of empty clam shells littering the area around the animal's lair. The octopus likes to eat its bivalved relatives in the safety of its home, after which their shells are unceremoniously tossed out the front door.

121. Map Cowrie *Cypraea mappa* Linnaeus ● Disk Algae *Rhipilia orientalis* A. & E. S. Geep ● Crustose Coralline Algae ● 1-1/3 times life size ● Ulach pass, Ngcheangel islands, Belau ● 21 meters ● 6 September 1971

Map cowries, like most cowries, are nocturnal. They rest under ledges during the day and emerge to forage only at night. Their polished shells are porcelain-smooth because they have a protective mantle which can be extended over the domed surface from both sides of the shells' ventral opening.

Some gastropods, like this cowrie, graze on rocky terrain, while other species eat soft corals. Other gastropods, such as tulip and cone shells, bury in the sand, emerging to feed at night. Early in the morning their grooved trails can be seen, weaving from point A to point B. At point B, usually where there is a hump of sand, the mollusk has resubmerged.

If you wish to collect live shells by looking for their trails, wear heavy gloves. If the mollusk is a cone shell do not dig for it with bare hands. Some cone shells are armed with miniature and highly venomous harpoons.

122. Thorny Oyster *Spondylus* sp. ● Coffee Lace Coral *Stylaster* sp. ● Life size ● Mbere reef, New Caledonia ● 23 meters ● 25 September 1965

The thorny oyster is actually a scallop. Unfortunately, the person who gave the animal its common name didn't know his shells.

These scallops, with their lovely variegated mantles, are much more beautiful than any shell specimen propped on a collector's bookshelf, the more so because these living animals are encrusted with more decorations than a Christmas gingerbread cookie.

The scallop has two rows of blue eyes lining the edges of its shell, all keeping watch on the existing light level. If a shadow or even a slight, unexpected displacement of water occurs, the two shells instantly snap shut.

123. Crimson Nudibranch *Ceratosoma cornigerum* Adams & Reeve ● 1-1/3 times life size ● Tanabe Bay, Shirahama, Wakayama-ken, Japan ● 10 meters ● 19 June 1966

In a world of many favored subjects, nudibranchs are one of my most favored. These shelless snails are exceedingly beautiful, though other animals which they feed upon, such as sponges, bryozoans, and even cerianthid anemones, might not agree. One species of nudibranch will go right down the hole in pursuit of a retracted cerianthid despite the anemone's stinging nematocysts. In fact nudibranchs are able to digest some nematocyst-bearing animals without triggering their weapons. The nematocysts are then positioned just under the surface of the nudibranch's skin, still armed for the mollusk's own protection.

125. American Lobster *Homarus americanus* H. Milne Edwards ● Crustose Coralline Algae ● Life size ● Hodgkins Cove, Cape Ann, Massachusetts, U.S.A. ● 6 meters ● 31 August 1967

The American or Maine lobster is endowed with two fore claws, one of which is the big crusher in contrast to its counterpart which is designed for more delicate work. This arrangement must be useful, for some crabs and shrimps have fore claws of varying design, serving different functions.

Like many of the cold-water invertebrates, lobsters are also active during the day. However, their activity increases around evening when they wander farther from home in search of a meal which may even include another lobster.

Like humans, lobsters like to eat, among other things, crabs and lobsters. Like humans, lobsters do not particularly hold in reverence their own kind.

126. Jonah Crabs *Cancer borealis* Stimpson • Algae • Life size • Hodgkins Cove, Cape Ann, Massachusetts, U.S.A. • 6 meters • 29 August 1967

At the end of summer in Hodgkins Cove, I came across a pair of Jonah crabs. The female had just molted, and her cast-off shell lay upside down in front of them. The male crab was above her, protecting her. Alone, she would have been defenseless, since her new pink shell was still soft. However, when the female molts, Jonah crabs mate. As long as the pair stay together during this time, her individual survival and the propagation of the species are doubly served. The female Jonah crab carries her fertilized eggs about with her, attached to the swimmerets under her abdomen. When the eggs finally hatch, the tiny zoeae float to the surface and drift with the currents as plankton. After four or five days, if they survive, they sink to the bottom, where they are ready to molt for the first time.

127. Pederson Cleaning Shrimp *Periclimenes pedersoni* Chace • Spiral Anemone *Bartholomea annulata* (Lesueur) • Little Star Coral *Montastrea annularis* (Ellis & Solander) • 1-1/3 times life size • Mastic Cay reef, Andros Island, Bahamas • 6 meters • 13 August 1968

One way to avoid predators is to be of service to them and, at the same time, have a home of anemone tentacles to retreat to when a fish, more hungry than harried, approaches. Like the clownfishes, quite a number of shrimps live with sea anemones, and most of them pick parasites off fishes to eat. The little shrimps swim out from the anemone and signal to an approaching fish by waving their long white antennae. If the fish is bothered by its parasites it stops, spreads its fins, and tilts its body in such a way that the shrimps know the fish wants to be cleaned. The shrimps then climb on the fish and begin their parasite hunt like children combing the yard on Easter morning.

128. Blue Crab *Callinectes sapidus* Rathbun • Ragged Sea Hare *Bursatella plei* Gray • Tube Worms • Algae • Life size • Port Largo, Upper Key Largo, Florida, U.S.A. • 5 meters • 24 April 1969

Blue crabs relish the internal parts of ragged sea hares, which they pull out of the dying victim like spaghetti—some in the mouth, some on the plate, and some in between.

Blue crabs avoid predators such as octopuses, but with their own strength and greater mobility, they look to the more sluggish creatures for their food supply. Some scientists believed that the purple ink rising from the sea hare is a substance released for self-defense. Ragged sea hares always release this ink when disturbed, but obviously the purple fluid seems not to deter this feeding crab.

129. Bulldozer Shrimp *Alpheus djiboutensis* DeMan • Lookout Goby *Cryptocentrus lutheri* Klausewitz • 1-1/4 times life size • Kesebekuu pass reef, Mekeald lagoon, Ngeruktabel island, Belau • 6 meters • 10 September 1969

This odd couple live together in a hole in the sand that the shrimp builds and keeps free of debris. The goby is the lookout at the entrance to their home, while the shrimp bulldozes sand away from the hole. The shrimp merely lowers its fore claws and proceeds forward, pushing sand fifteen to twenty-five centimeters from the entrance and releasing it. The claws are then raised and, like a bulldozer, the animal goes into reverse and begins again.

When disturbed, both shrimp and goby back into their hole. Their movements in and out of the hole cause minor sand slides, which keep the shrimp perpetually busy. While all this work goes on, the goby watches and periodically engulfs a mouthful of sand, vibrates its cheeks to filter the limestone grains through its gills for tiny organisms to eat. The shrimp may feed while it is bulldozing the sand. Small creatures living there are exposed by the shrimp's work.

Very often a pair of gobies and a pair of shrimps inhabit the same hole. Since corals and many other encrusting animals cannot take hold on the shifting grains of sand, there are large desertlike expanses of sand on the back reef. Here the goby and shrimp community resides, their holes dotting the bottom a few meters apart. If their residences were too close together, each "family" would not have enough to eat.

130. Slipper Lobster *Scyllarides astori* Holthuis • 2/3 life size • Daphne Island, Galápagos Islands, Ecuador • 12 meters • 29 April 1973

In the cooler currents of the Galápagos and Japan, slipper lobsters are active during the day. In the tropics a diver will see them only at night, for they are much more secretive than the spiny lobsters. They hide deep within the caves and winding passages of the reef. They are generally smaller than the spiny lobsters and, unlike them, do not have thorny horns over their eyes, or large spiked antennae for armament. The smaller species are eaten regularly by some reef fishes which inhabit deep water, but the shells of slipper lobsters do provide a measure of protection.

131. New Caledonia Slipper Lobster *Parribacus caledonicus* Holthuis • Life size • The Great Reef, Bailechesengel island, Ngemelis islands, Belau • 6 meters • 27 August 1974

The scientific name of this nocturnal slipper lobster indicates that it lives in New Caledonia. However, this individual was photographed on a moonlit reef in Belau, proof that it also ranges the western equatorial Pacific region.

There are many slipper lobster species, some large (up to 30 centimeters in length) and others only a few centimeters long. They come in many shapes, colors, and patterns. These two are colored similarly to their surroundings. The color and pattern of the New Caledonia slipper lobster is patterned to match the reef, even though the colors (revealed by the flash) are different. On a moonlit night only another New Caledonia slipper lobster is expected to recognize the difference.

132. Giant Barnacle *Balanus nubilus* Darwin • Shrimp • Crustose Coralline Algae • Bryozoans • Anemones • 1-1/3 times life size • North Coast, Port Walter Entrance, Baranof Island, Alaska, U.S.A. • 12 meters • 27 June 1972

Barnacles may resemble mollusks, which they were once thought to be, since they have a shelled structure and are sessile—some growing on rocky areas like oysters. However, their jointed body segments show that barnacles are crustaceans, a discovery made during studies of their life history. Their planktonic stages revealed their crustacean heritage.

When I made this photograph, I thought it amusing that one crustacean, the tiny shrimp, had found a home in another crustacean, the old barnacle "shell." These shrimps also live on the elongated column of an arctic sea anemone, taking shelter beneath a brightly colored sunburst of tentacles.

133. Green Crab *Carcinus maenas* (Linnaeus) • Green Sea Urchins *Strongylocentrotus droebachiensis* (Müller) • Kelp • Life size • Benjamin River, Sedgwick, Maine, U.S.A. • 10 meters • 23 August 1967

Although shrimps, lobsters, and crabs are burdened with an external skeleton which must be shed before continued growth can take place, they have nevertheless adapted to their world in the sea. They are vulnerable during that short time between shells, but generally have a good measure of protection from many predators. If they lose a claw in a fight or during an escape, they are able to regrow the lost appendage after a few molts.

Crustaceans are related to insects and half of all the animals on our planet that roam the skies, the lands, the seas, and all those many realms where water meets land and land meets sky.

135. Rainbow Sea Star *Asterias vulgaris* Verrill • Green Sea Urchins *Strongylocentrotus droebachiensis* (Müller) • Brown mussels *Modiolus modiolus* (Linnaeus) • 1-1/2 times life size • Hodgkins Cove, Cape Ann, Massachusetts, U.S.A. • 5 meters • 31 August 1967

This rainbow sea star inhabits the northeastern coast of the United States, and the North Atlantic. Its scientific name, *asterias vulgaris*, signifies its abundance, but the name disturbs me when its more modern meaning is implied. The Latin word *vulgaris* has been used for many plants and animals, and scientists have perhaps unthinkingly perpetuated the idea of the common as vulgar.

This rainbow sea star is equally lovely whether arrayed in pinks and purples, amber, or yellow-oranges. In their element, sea stars virtually glow with life, making them the very antithesis of anything common—or vulgar.

136. Rose Sea Star *Crossaster papposus* (Linnaeus) • Autumn Sea Urchin *Strongylocentrotus polyacanthus* Agassiz & Clark • Kelp • 1-1/4 times life size • Dock, Constantine Harbor, Amchitka Island, Alaska, U.S.A. • 20 meters • 11 July 1972

Sea stars and other echinoderms such as sea urchins and sea cucumbers have a unique water circulatory system. This "water vascular system," as it is called, is essential to the animal's ability to move, to defend itself, to feed, to excrete wastes, to maintain body shape in some instances, and to breathe. Sessile sponges make the same use of seawater in a less specialized way, but sea stars and sea urchins utilize the hydraulic property of water to move their many tube feet.

In a world greatly perpetuated and fed by plankton, mobility might not seem absolutely necessary for survival, but when an animal can move, it can occupy a new world and it has the potential for feeding on other forms of life. In the brief summer of the perpetually cold Aleutian depths, the autumn sea urchins are eating circles out of a deceased kelp frond, while the rose sea star grazes tiny organisms from its surface.

137. Pin Cushion Sea Star *Culcita novaeguineae* Müller & Troschel • Life size • Jellyfish Cove I, Risong, Ngeruptachel island, Belau • 5 meters • 3 July 1971

It may appear that this sea star has no arms, but if it is quickly turned over, a diver can watch the rows of tube feet retracting into the animal's flattened ventral surface. Sea stars can right themselves if they tumble over on their backs, and I have photographed sequences of them and have watched how their arms are bent around to place the animals' tube feet on firm footing. Since the pin cushion sea star is nearly round, I thought the animal would have difficulty righting itself. I was wrong. The animal righted itself about as quickly as it takes a sea star with arms to accomplish the task. The pin cushion sea star creases its body across its ventral surface until one of its rows of tube feet comes into contact with the bottom. Then the tube feet begin to walk while the animal continues to fold over on itself until its dorsal surface is upright again.

138. Dappled Sea Cucumber *Stichopus* sp. ● Crinoid, Sponges, Tube Corals, Lace Ascidians ● 2/3 life size ● The Great Reef, Bailechesengel island, Ngemelis islands, Belau ● 14 meters ● 5 July 1973

This nocturnal sea cucumber emerges only at night to feed on the reef. Its dappled colors remind me of Gerard Manley Hopkins' poem "Pied Beauty."

> Glory be to God for dappled things—
> For skies of couple-colour as a brinded cow;
> For rose-moles all in stipple upon trout that swim;
> Fresh-firecoal chestnut-falls; finches' wings;
> Landscape plotted and pieced—fold, fallow, and plough;
> And áll trádes, their gear and tackle and trim.
>
> All things counter, original, spare, strange;
> Whatever is fickle, freckled (who knows how?)
> With swift, slow; sweet, sour; adazzle, dim;
> He fathers-forth whose beauty is past change:
> Praise him.

139. Ten-fingered Sea Cucumber *Cucumaria frondosa* (Gunnerus) ● Green Sea Urchins *Strongylocentrotus droebachiensis* (Müller) ● Life size ● Benjamin River, Sedgwick, Maine, U.S.A. ● 10 meters ● 23 August 1967

Many tropical sea cucumbers are not as active as this cold-water beauty. Its bushy fingers collect plankton with clocklike regularity, stuffing one plankton-laden finger after another into its central mouth where the plankton is removed. Approximately every thirty seconds a finger is withdrawn and another engulfed. An observer can sense the eagerness with which this animal feeds itself.

140. Club-spined Sea Urchin *Eucidaris thouarsii* (Valenciennes) ● Tube Corals and Calcareous Algae ● 1-1/4 times life size ● Cousin's Rock, Santiago Island, Galápagos Islands, Ecuador ● 11 meters ● 2 May 1973

Sea urchins are endowed with a variety of spines, long or short, thin or fat, with or without venom. This club-spined urchin moves about on the bottom. The clubs function as jaw-breaking obstructions to predators, in contrast to those of other species that function as sharp lances. The enlarged surfaces of these clubs provide living space for encrusting life which also inhabits the steep, rocky face of the surrounding submarine terrain.

141. Short-spined Sea Urchin *Tripneustes gratilla* (Linnaeus) ● Life size ● Tanabe Bay, Shirahama, Wakayama-ken, Japan ● 8 meters ● 16 June 1966

A few of the many tube feet of this sea urchin are more easily seen extending from beneath the animal's body. Unlike sea stars and sea cucumbers, most sea urchins have a rigid skeleton, or "test," hidden beneath a battery of spines. An urchin is easily associated with its spines because they are so prominent. But they are only the animal's armament. Hidden from view, the test houses the animal. It is formed of ten double rows of delicate, curved calcium carbonate plates, intricately joined together. The "tubercles" on the plates to which the spines are attached add to the beauty of the test, which also has symmetrical rows of tiny holes to facilitate the passage of water to and from the tube feet. The many different urchin skeletons are as beautiful as the structure of snowflakes. They have an elegance all their own.

142. Red Sea Urchin *Strongylocentrotus franciscanus* (Agassiz) ● Barnacles ● Life size ● Dodd Narrows, Mudge Island, Vancouver Island, B.C., Canada ● 8 meters ● 16 November 1969

There are more than 860 known living species of urchins and sand dollars. These bottom dwellers range from low-tide level to depths of more than 5000 meters. The test is flexible in a number of these deep-water forms, in distinct contrast to sand dollars, which are more skeleton and spines than flesh.

Sea otters feed on some sea urchins, as do triggerfishes in the Caribbean and humans in Japan and many Pacific islands. Urchins, in turn, feed on seaweed, organic matter in the mud and sand, animal remains, and even on sand dollars. I once encountered a group of sea stars and sea urchins ringed around a sand dollar, feasting away, echinoderms all.

143. Autumn Sea Urchins *Strongylocentrotus polyacanthus* Agassiz & Clark ● Life size ● Dock, Constantine Harbor, Amchitka Island, Alaska, U.S.A. ● 20 meters ● 10 July 1972

These lovely little creatures, living in Aleutian waters, are like starry ornaments adorning a Christmas tree. This photograph recalled to me the meaning of urchin, those street urchins, little waifs already on their own in the world. I wonder who had memories of old London's streets when he named these animals urchins of the sea.

144. Feather Crinoid *Lamprometra parmata parmata* (Müller) ● Coral ● Life size ● Nature Reserve, Gulf of Aqaba, Eilat, Israel ● 6 meters ● 1 April 1965

Feather crinoids and their close relatives, the deep-water sea lilies, number more than 800 living species. The sea lilies are stalked—anchored to the bottom—while the more-shallow-water feather stars are freed (beyond youth) to move about. Some, like this one, hide under ledges or in caves during the day and emerge only at dusk to feed on plankton riding the night tide. Others, like the one photographed in the Loyalty Islands, remain in one place and spread their feathery arms to feed. When mealtime is over, at slack tide, the many arms slowly roll up into tight coils.

145. Feather Crinoid ● Life size ● Point Merlet reef, Lifou, Loyalty Islands ● 21 meters ● 3 September 1965

Crinoids, like the nautiluses, are "living fossils." Their essential structure has changed very little over millions of years. Like the nautiluses they, also, were much more abundant when the earth was younger. More than 5000 fossil species have been described, representing 750 genera. The fossil crinoids are actually better known than the living species. Their skeletons, excavated by scientists, were more easily studied than their living descendants who have now survived long enough to be observed by *Homo aquatius*.

147. Fairy Basslet *Gramma loreto* Poey ● Star Coral *Montastrea cavernosa* (Linnaeus) ● 1-1/4 times life size ● White Point outer reef, Hog Island, Bay Islands, Honduras ● 12 meters ● 14 September 1964

Here are two life forms living together in the sea. The star coral, like most of the animals I have discussed, is an invertebrate. Its skeleton has evolved from an animal which inhabited the shallow ocean floor. Over millions of years it acquired the ability to construct its own base, its own house—internalized. Through time, as it reproduced itself, colonies arose with homes joined together like an apartment complex fulfilling the inhabitants' needs.

However, the sea-floor world was limited, and as space became more scarce, some organisms rediscovered the less crowded open water. Thus the vertebrates arose by slowly experimenting with the properties of water and the dynamics of movement within it. Eventually these "fishes" could hover in mid-water by adjusting the volume of air in their swim bladders to attain neutral buoyancy. This fairy basslet amply demonstrates the virtues of the swim bladder, coupled with the animal's vertebrate skeleton. It can hover "right" side up over a coral colony, or "right" side down under a coral ledge. It can float in any position and orient itself to whatever it chooses. Its bones, muscles, and fins are designed for ease and quickness of movement in the water.

148. Golden Longnose Butterflyfish *Chelmon rostratus* (Linnaeus) ● Tube Corals, Red Sponge, and Algae ● Life size ● Cyclone Point reef, Heron Island, Queensland, Australia ● 10 meters ● 5 October 1965

The swim bladder enables many reef fishes to have vertically compressed bodies. Sharks do not have swim bladders, and their bodies are horizontally flattened on their ventral surface to create lift and minimize sinking. In contrast this golden long-nose butterflyfish is highly compressed vertically. Its design is oriented to the greater ease and quickness of movement around coral formations which would prove too much of an obstacle course for a shark.

Like many of the butterflyfishes this one has a black false-eye spot near its tail, to mislead the butterflyfish's enemies. A predator, anticipating the forward movement of its victim in the same way that a hunter leads a bird in flight, ordinarily strikes at the head. On several occasions I have seen a butterflyfish with a gouge near the eye spot, evidence that some predator attacked the wrong end, giving the butterflyfish a better opportunity to escape. Since the butterflyfish is often quite intent on looking for food, the false-eye is, in a sense, a kind of lookout for the rest of the body.

149. Golden Boxfish *Ostracion tuberculatus* Linnaeus ● Pink Tube Corals, Ascidians, Sponges, and Algae ● Life size ● Cyclone Point reef, Heron Island, Queensland, Australia ● 11 meters ● 6 October 1965

The fundamental feeding habits of fishes are linked to the shapes and sizes of their mouths. Parrotfish teeth are made for scraping, a grouper's large mouth for gulping, while the tiny mouths of butterflyfishes reflect their dainty feeding habits. This golden boxfish is also a dainty feeder, at least compared with a shark. These diverse anatomical structures reveal the many ways fishes have evolved and in the process survived.

150. Freckled Grouper *Epinephelus coatesi* (Whitley) ● Life size ● Mutremdiu point, Uchelbeluu reef, Belau ● 14 meters ● 4 July 1971

Different clans and villages in Belau have gods which must not be killed. The yellow-lip sea snake is the god of one village. Another village god is the green turtle. The god of one clan is the brown moray eel. The village god of Ngchesar on Babeldaob is the spotted eagle ray. If any one from Ngchesar kills an eagle ray, that person or a member of the family will die. If a man accidentally harms or kills an eagle ray, he or a member of his family must go to the woman of the village who is responsible for the god. The woman must be paid with Belauan money to rectify the offense. This woman, within whom the god dwells, is clairvoyant and can actually tell the offender when, where, and how he killed the god. I was told by a man from Ngchesar that when this old woman dies, the god will leave her body and enter another woman of the same clan.

I had given up spear fishing many years ago and only occasionally speared for a meal. However, when I decided not to rely solely on photography and writing to earn a living, I began to spear fish for food. After relating to fishes as friends for so many years, I was suddenly confronted with the unsublimated hunter part of myself, which took a measure of delight in the kill, though a different layer of my being recoiled at the slaughter. Soon I decided to have a god, some animal which I could not kill. I chose the freckled grouper.

151. Golden Cardinalfish *Archamia fucata* (Cantor) ● **Black Coral** *Antipathes* sp. ● 1-1/3 times life size ● The Creek, Red Sea, Obhor Kuraa, Saudi Arabia ● 15 meters ● 4 March 1965

Many small reef fishes, including these golden cardinalfish, hover among the branches of stony corals, gorgonians, and black corals. Small fishes are vulnerable to many larger ones with bigger mouths. Various groupers feed on their neighbors. Thus a network of coral branches is an important part of the continued well-being of many small reef fishes.

152. Longspine Squirrelfish *Holocentrotus rufus* Walbaum ● **Elkhorn Coral** *Acropora palmata* (Lamarck) ● Life size ● Hog Island, Bay Islands, Honduras ● 1 meter ● 9 September 1964

This Caribbean squirrelfish was surprised while resting between the massive branches of an elkhorn coral. Apprehension is mingled with curiosity at the sight of a strange intruder. On a reef rarely frequented by man, fishes and other animals are quite unafraid and will actually swim toward a diver to get a closer look. In areas where divers hunt fishes and other animals, such as turtles, the animals will swim away or retreat to coral hideaways. The most hunted fishes react the fastest when a diver approaches them.

When this squirrelfish is alarmed, it emits a rapid grunting sound to signal its distress. Most wounded fishes send out distress signals which attract sharks within seconds. When photographing, it is wise to avoid alarming fishes that may signal the sharks.

153. Brown Clownfish *Amphiprion bicinctus* Rüppell ● **Sea Anemone** *Radianthus* sp. ● 1-1/2 times life size ● The Creek, Red Sea, Obhor Kuraa, Saudi Arabia ● 15 meters ● 15 March 1965

Scientists are still not certain what prevents an anemone's stinging nematocysts from being triggered when a clownfish touches them. However, it is known that when a clownfish is experimentally separated from its anemone for several months and then reintroduced, the fish must reacclimate itself by touching parts of its body to the anemone before it is able to swim freely among the tentacles. The clownfish first hovers above a tentacle and brushes it with its tail fin. In time the clownfish touches more and more of its body against the tentacles. It is thought that the fish acquires an identifying slime from the anemone, for any fish not coated with anemone slime triggers the nematocysts and is killed.

It is also likely that the clownfish's familiarity and subsequent lack of fear communicate to the anemone its normal mode of life as symbiont. Needless to say, no cerebral receptivity exists in the anemone. It is more likely that a behavioral communication exists between them in addition to their chemocommunication.

How clownfishes interact with anemones is equally important, for those fishes were once strangers to anemones, and each new generation in its early life is a stranger to the anemone. Clownfish eggs are attached on a cleared coral rock at the base of the anemone's column. After hatching, these tiny fish begin a new association, perhaps aided by their parents.

154. Pine Cone Fish *Monocentris japonicus* (Houttuyn) ● **Algae** ● Life size ● Tanabe Bay, Shirahama, Wakayama-ken, Japan ● 10 meters ● 5 June 1966

Animals live in the deepest depths of the ocean, but life did not begin there. Over hundreds of millions of years animals gradually migrated and are still migrating to the depths from the shallow sunlit waters. The abyss has become home to many creatures. So well adapted are they to it that many have evolved their own bioluminescent lights to aid them in the eternal night of their world.

One animal "between worlds" is this adult pine cone fish which was removed from an aquarium and photographed in shallow water. The tiny round juveniles live six to ten meters down under ledges in the company of long-spined sea urchins. When the juveniles grow older they migrate to deeper water. The adults definitely look like inhabitants of the deep, and proof of their life-style is a bioluminescent light organ located on each side of their lower jaw.

155. Mangrove Snapper *Lutjanus argentimaculatus* (Forskål) ● 2/3 life size ● Jellyfish Marine Lake, Oreor island, Belau ● 4 meters ● 31 August 1969

Testimony to the success of plankton is the presence of this mangrove snapper in an interior marine lake of Belau. The long winding tunnels leading from the lagoon to the lake would be hazardous, if not impossible, for an adult snapper to navigate. There are very few species of fishes in the lake, a specialized community. The mangrove snapper larva was able to survive in the lake because of its adaptability to brackish water environments. Considerable numbers of plankton journey through the intertidal tunnels each day, but all those plants and animals, ill-fitted to the marine lake environment, perish.

156. Stoplight Parrotfish *Sparisoma viride* Bonnaterre ● **Remora** *Echeneis naucrates* Linnaeus ● 2/3 life size ● Molasses Reef, Upper Key Largo, Florida, U.S.A. ● 11 meters ● 29 June 1967

The remora or shark sucker does not confine its life entirely to sharks. Juveniles often live in the gill cavities of swordfish and sailfish where they dine on some of the food which their host captures. They also live with manta and eagle rays, turtles, and medium-size fishes such as this stoplight parrotfish. Some animals are not unduly bothered by the presence of the remora and even seem to enjoy its company, but the stoplight parrotfish appears to resent the intrusion. Juvenile remoras have a host problem somewhat comparable to the house problem of a hermit crab. As each grows, each must find a bigger host or house. A parrotfish will often try to extricate himself from a remora, and a diver sometimes acts as a means to that end. If a remora decides to leave the parrotfish and swim to the diver, the parrot quickly swims away. When the remora discovers that the diver is not quite suitable to its needs, it also swims away to look for another host. It is not uncommon to encounter a solitary remora looking for a host.

157. Bridled Burrfish *Chilomycterus antennatus* (Cuvier) ● **Turtle Grass** *Thalassia testudinum* ● **Manatee Grass** *Cymodocea* sp. ● Life size ● White Rock Bank, Upper Key Largo, Florida, U.S.A. ● 3 meters ● 4 July 1967

Some fishes rely on speed or wing-shaped fins to fly out of the water when pursued by another fish intent on making a meal of them. The bridled burrfish is no open water skip jack or flying fish. He paddles around coral heads and frequents turtle grasses looking for small crabs and other diminutive organisms to eat. If disturbed by a diver, the burrfish may scuttle off to a coral grotto, but if no retreat is available, he gulps in water and his body inflates to several times its normal size. If this is not enough to frighten a predator, the gentle animal is armed with a multitude of spines designed to dull most appetites.

158. Emperor Angelfish *Pomacanthus imperator* (Bloch) ● 2/3 life size ● Ngerumekaol pass reef, Ulong island, Belau ● 14 meters ● 27 June 1971

The emperor angel is one of the most exquisitely patterned fish on a Pacific coral reef blessed with many contenders for the title. I would imagine that, in a world where colors and patterns are so abundant, reef life has become something of an evolutionary beauty contest. If man is so beauty-conscious, why should we be surprised if other animals are equally cognizant of "style"?

159. Emperor Sea Bass *Variola louti* (Forskål) ● **Platter Staghorn Coral** *Acropora* sp. ● 1/2 life size ● Mbere reef, New Caledonia ● 14 meters ● 17 September 1965

In a family album of fishes only a photograph of the emperor sea bass could be pasted on the same page with that of an emperor angel. The emperor sea bass is rivaled for beauty among its kind only by the smallest fairy basslets. The other groupers and sea basses might, were they capable, feel that they are to the emperor sea bass what a peacock's feet are to its plumage.

161. Neon Goby *Gobiosoma oceanops* (Jordan) ● **Spotted Sea Bass** *Epinephelus itajara* (Lichtenstein) ● 3/4 life size ● Patch reef, Lower Matecumbe Key, Florida, U.S.A. ● 5 meters ● 18 July 1965

There are full-time cleaners, part-time cleaners, and certain fishes which only pick parasites off other fishes when young. As the part-time cleaners grow, their feeding habits change to fulfill their increased body size and stomach capacity. A juvenile French angelfish feeds on the ectoparasites of other fishes, but as it grows it mixes its diet, feeding increasingly on sponges. As an adult it no longer services other fishes.

The neon goby, which only grows to about five centimeters, is very nearly a full-time cleaner. It has a "cleaning station" to which other fishes, such as this spotted sea bass, come to have their parasites removed. The cleaning habit may have begun with some interaction between small-size fishes and shrimps, and the large fishes that shared coral ledges and caves. A large fish is equally a part of the environment as a small fish, an environment to be explored for food. As the relationships become more and more purposeful, with each partner assuming more of a role, certain shrimps and fishes were able to stay at home and receive periodic visits from those they cleaned.

162. Black and Blue Cleaner Wrasse *Labroides dimidiatus* (Cuvier & Valenciennes) ● Autumn-fire Goatfish *Parupeneus* sp. ● Mountain Coral *Porites lutea* Milne Edwards & Haime ● 2/3 life size ● Bulari Pass, New Caledonia ● 15 meters ● 2 February 1963

A perfect example of the great importance and degree to which cleaning has evolved is this congregation of goatfishes filling the wrasse's waiting room. They have come to its cleaning station the way patients come to a doctor's office. Most of them have their fins and barbels folded in marked contrast to the erect fins and extended barbels of the goatfish being cleaned. It is possible that not all the goatfish need servicing, but since they travel as a school, they accompany the patients to the doctor's office, like attendant relatives.

163. Salmon-backed Cleaner Wrasses *Labroides rubrolabiatus* Randall ● Pink Fairy Bass *Mirolabrichthys tuka* Herre ● Porous Coral *Porites iwayamaensis* Eguchi? ● 2/3 life size ● Tuanoa Pass, Tahiti, Society Islands ● 8 meters ● 2 December 1962

Different labrid cleaner wrasses have assumed slightly different roles. In Tahiti there are three different species. The black and blue wrasse has a well-defined doctor's office. The salmon-backed wrasses have a less well-defined office, comparable to a hospital. The doctor covers several square meters of reef area. The adult bicolor wrasse travels even farther, servicing the larger community like a doctor on continual house call. These differing roles, though they may overlap, help to spread out the work and minimize competition.

164. White-lightning Cleaning Goby *Gobiosoma genie* Böhlke and Robins ● Spanish Hogfish *Bodianus rufus* (Linnaeus) ● Nassau Grouper *Epinephelus striatus* (Bloch) ● Life size ● The Barge, Small Hope Bay, Andros Island, Bahamas ● 21 meters ● 12 August 1968

Since the doctors are usually small, it is not unusual to see two or more of them performing their services simultaneously on the same patient. Some are pairs and families. As inhabitants of the same coral niche they share the work like a team of doctors and nurses in an operating room, though each works on its own without assistance.

Here, three gobies and a juvenile Spanish hogfish are sharing the work. The gobies are full-time cleaners while only juvenile Spanish hogfish function as doctors. The adult hogfish have the delicate touch necessary to operate on their patients without harming them.

165. Black and Blue Cleaner Wrasse *Labroides dimidiatus* (Cuvier & Valenciennes) ● Blue-spotted Sea Bass *Plectropomus maculatus* (Bloch) ● 2/3 life size ● Cyclone Point reef, Heron Island, Queensland, Australia ● 11 meters ● 15 October 1965

Tropical Indo-Pacific waters are populated with five known labrid cleaners. These wrasses are the full-time doctors to the fish community. They even clean each other. The *Labroides dimidiatus* is by far the most abundant and widespread member of the group. It is always eager to perform its services even on divers whose interest it mistakes for a willingness to be cleaned. Their body markings distinguish them from other fishes. They and their patients have become so accustomed to their mutually beneficial roles that a black and blue wrasse can enter the mouth of a blue-spotted sea bass to pick parasites with no fear of being eaten. Like other patients, the sea bass extends its gills to facilitate cleaning. The gill rakers are easily visible in this photograph. When the wrasse is finished doctoring, it may exit the patient's mouth through one or the other of the gill openings.

166. Bicolor Cleaner Wrasse *Labroides bicolor* Fowler & Bean ● Squirrelfish *Myripristis pralinius* (Cuvier & Valenciennes) ● 1-1/3 times life size ● Mutremdiu point, Uchelbeluu reef, Belau ● 14 meters ● 27 June 1971

The color patterns of the juvenile labrid wrasses are a combination of black and electric purple, blue or yellow. All the juveniles live under ledges and do not roam very far. Often they live with a group of squirrelfish whom they service during the day while the squirrels are resting up for their nightly activities.

Though these juvenile doctors are quite small, their striking colors enable them to be recognized easily and to perform their services without being harmed. Since they do not greatly compete with the adult cleaners, or with one another, their colors are somewhat uniform from one species to the next. Only as they grow and assume different roles do their colors become different.

167. Peppermint Cleaner Shrimp *Hippolysmata grabhami* Gordon ● Orange Fairy Basses *Anthias squamipinnis* (Peters) ● 1-1/3 times life size ● Nature Reserve, Gulf of Aqaba, Eilat, Israel ● 6 meters ● 29 March 1965

Cleaning symbiosis is one of the most obvious examples of how interrelated are the sea's inhabitants. As we already know, many small shrimp live in some association with quite a number of different animals, including clams, sea stars, and anemones. There are many species of cleaner shrimps. Some species live in groups of six to eight and virtually surround a patient when approached. The smallest shrimp are naturals as cleaners.

One of the most widespread doctors is the peppermint cleaner shrimp. It lives singly or in pairs under coral ledges. Here, one is perched on a small promontory ministering to an orange fairy bass. Deftly it removes and eats the parasitic copepods from the body of the fish. Inasmuch as copepods are crustaceans like the shrimp, the cleaner and cleaned have a greater degree of affinity than do the two crustaceans, unless affinity is measured by the closeness that exists when copepods are in the shrimp's stomach. California cleaner shrimps are neither fully adapted to cleaning nor distinctively marked with white antennae as a signal to their patients. These interns are not immune to predation. Occasionally an intern ends up in a patient's stomach.

168. Yellow-tailed Cleaner Wrasses *Diproctacanthus xanthurus* Randall ● String Sponge *Xestospongia exiqua* (Kirkpatrick) ● Life size ● Kesebekuu pass reef, Mekeald lagoon, Ngeruktabel island, Belau ● 4 meters ● 6 September 1969

Not all cleaner wrasses are labrids. In the Caribbean the juveniles of the blue head wrasse clean. A number of other fishes, including other wrasses in the Indo-Pacific, clean. These yellow-tailed wrasses swim over a reef flat and service fishes.

Generally those fishes that do clean full-time are marked with stripes and bright colors (usually yellow or blue—colors easily seen underwater). They also swim in an undulating up-and-down motion. This photograph shows the up-and-down positions of the swimming movement. Many of the sea's creatures express this poetry of motion.

169. Black and Blue Cleaner Wrasse *Labroides dimidiatus* (Cuvier & Valenciennes) ● Squirrelfish *Holocentrus sammara* (Forskål) ● 3/4 life size ● Amédée Island reef, New Caledonia ● 3 meters ● 22 January 1963

Probably I will never forget completely the circumstances surrounding many of my favorite photographs. I am certain I will not forget this photograph. The depth was only three meters, the water was calm, and I was snorkeling. Each time I dived to photograph the black and blue wrasse and the squirrelfish, the patients would become nervous and signal to the wrasse to stop cleaning operations. I decided that the only way to photograph them was to dive and lie on the bottom until they relaxed and cleaning commenced. I had to be patient, however; they had gills and I didn't. My lungs were soon screaming for a breath of fresh air. Fortunately the moment arrived to make this photograph. No sooner did the flash bulb ignite than I rocketed to the surface like a polaris missile.

171. Yellow-lip Sea Snake *Laticauda colubrina* (Schneider) ● Staghorn Coral *Acropora* sp. ● Life size ● Amédée Island reef, New Caledonia ● 1 meter ● 20 August 1965

For those accustomed to land snakes, it seems strange to watch a snake traversing a coral formation, nosing in small crevices, looking for tiny fishes. It seems even more unreal to descend 45 meters to a deep reef and come upon a sea snake asleep under a coral, or ascending to the surface far above. Would that I could dive as deep and stay as long.

All sea snakes are deadly poisonous. Some are aggressive, especially at mating season. Others, such as the yellow-lip, are gentle. Some islanders wrap them around their arms and neck, but nonetheless these snakes are extremely venomous. Most accidents occur precisely because people handle them without proper precaution.

Humans, of course, are relatively new to the sea, and any dangers which await them were not specifically designed for their discomfort, though man himself is really the most dangerous marine organism. A diver can feel quite secure in the shallow seas with no more defense than his knowledge of marine animals, their behavior, and a measure of good sense.

172. Formosa Jellyfish *Olindioides formosa* Goto ● Life size ● Tanabe Bay, Shirahama, Wakayama-ken, Japan ● 15 meters ● 5 June 1966

As we have seen, many marine animals are able to defend themselves or at least avoid predators enough to survive. The animals in this section of the book are not singled out for any "ten most wanted" list, though a diver may want to avoid them. My purpose in assembling a gallery of marine life under dangerous animals is to give the uninformed some understanding of marine animal defense mechanisms so that the only defense a diver needs is recognition and avoidance.

This jellyfish, like many others, has tentacles armed with powerful nematocysts. Inasmuch as jellyfishes are 95 percent water, some of the organization that remains is, of necessity, needed for defense and food getting. Since a jellyfish could easily be torn apart by a struggling fish, the venom must be quick acting and painful enough to repel or stun predators and prey.

The sea wasp off northeastern Australia has reached the ultimate in this technology. An adult sea wasp can kill a man several minutes after contact. All the other jellyfishes are on a sliding scale downward from the sea wasp. I have no idea where the Formosa jellyfish is located on the scale because I was wearing rubber gloves when I touched it. Consequently our encounter in Japan's Inland Sea is remembered with fondness.

173. Crown-of-thorns Sea Star *Acanthaster planci* (Linnaeus) ● 1-1/3 times life size ● Amédée Island reef, New Caledonia ● 3 meters ● 9 September 1965

The crown-of-thorns sea star is well named. Each spine is tipped with a sharp venomous spike which penetrates the flesh and breaks off. The venom is very painful, at least to humans. Wounds become easily infected. The flesh can swell up and become hardened like a large callous.

But the crown-of-thorns is not immune from sea predators. During intensive investigations several years ago, scientists discovered that the triton trumpet, a large gastropod with a beautiful shell much valued by collectors, feeds on the crown-of-thorns. Both the sea star and the mollusk are nocturnal, feeding at night. When the triton trumpet locates a crown-of-thorns, it slides aboard while pushing the thorns aside with its tough, slippery foot. When atop the sea star, the trumpet shell extends its proboscus and injects a venom into the crown-of-thorn's flesh. When the animal is subdued, the triton trumpet begins to feast. A beautiful little shrimp also preys upon the crown-of-thorns, and during the early stages of its life many of the reef creatures feed on it. Scientists have theorized that intensive collection of triton trumpets as well as other crown-of-thorn predators, and the disruption of the normal reef community by blasting and dredging have perhaps given the crown-of-thorns an edge on its competitors, resulting in its population explosion.

174. Kidako Moray Eel *Gymnothorax kidako* (Schlegel) ● **Banded Cleaner Shrimp** *Stenopus hispidus* (Oliver) ● Crustose Coralline Algae ● Life size ● Tanabe Bay, Shirahama, Wakayama-ken, Japan ● 10 meters ● 3 June 1966

Moray eels are certainly formidable-looking fish. Their sharp teeth and somewhat sinister "smiles" give us cause to be concerned for our safety. They open and close their mouths, inhaling water to breathe, and this rhythmic, almost hypnotic process tends to make us classify the moray eel as a villain.

It is true that moray eels are endowed with a fine set of teeth, which they obviously use to secure food and can use on humans when molested. However, they are equally intimidated by that man-fish which is much larger than they. Small moray eels are quite often afraid of divers and sometimes flee with much haste to the safety of a coral cave. The larger two-to-three-meter morays are less frightened by a man and, if attacked or molested, will fight back. I once encountered a large moray eel at Raiatea in the Society Islands. The eel was protruding from his cave thirty meters beneath the surface. I wanted to photograph him, as he was by far the largest moray I had ever seen. When I moved closer to take the picture, the image of the eel's head filled the viewing window of the camera. I suddenly decided not to go close enough to get the eel in focus for I was afraid he might strike out in self-defense. If the eel were to clamp his teeth into my arm and back into his cave, no effort on my part would prevail against his strength and leverage. A close-up photograph was not worth the risk so I backed away and left him in peace.

175. Stonefish *Synanceja verrucosa* Bloch & Schneider ● Algae ● Life size ● Vata Bay, Noumea, New Caledonia ● 1-1/2 meters ● 18 August 1965

The stonefishes, lionfishes, and scorpionfishes are all members of the scorpionfish family. They all have venomous spines, most prominently the dorsal spines. The potency of the venom varies from species to species, depending on the size and development of the venom gland. The stonefish is the most venomous family member and therefore probably the most venomous fish in the sea. It has thirteen dorsal, three anal, and two pelvic spines, all equipped with venom glands. Pressure on the end of a spine causes it to inject venom hypodermically into the predator.

A stonefish, as its name implies, looks like an algae-covered stone. Occasionally I have seen stonefish perched on dead coral, but more often they bury in the sand or mud, or hide under coral heads until nightfall, when they emerge to feed. Many of them, though not all, live in the shallows and are extremely difficult to see because they look so unlike a fish. For these reasons the animal is a potential hazard to divers or bathers. Throughout the tropical Indo-Pacific it is best not to wade around barefoot in

the shallows. Reportedly the pain from the venom is so great that the unfortunate victim screams and thrashes wildly about before losing consciousness. If the person does not die; months may pass before he recovers, and his general health may be affected for the rest of his life.

176. Pin Cushion Sea Urchin *Astropyga radiata* ● Crustose Coralline Algae ● Red Encrusting Sponge ● 1-1/3 times life size ● Kuabsngas point reef, Teongel pass, Ngeruktabel island, Belau ● 15 meters ● 7 November 1967

The venom glands and spines of stonefish are hidden by the animal's warty flesh. Not so in the pin cushion sea urchin. Its spines are clearly visible and serve as a protection. The spines are very brittle and easily break off in the skin of any animal coming in contact with them, whereupon a poisonous pigment in the spine produces a painful wound. The sea urchin may be colored and elaborately patterned to call attention to itself as a warning against potential predators. The animal feeds on small reef organisms, primarily at night.

177. Red Sea Lionfish *Pterois radiata* Cuvier ● Crustose Coralline Algae ● 2/3 life size ● The Creek, Red Sea, Obhor Kuraa, Saudi Arabia ● 20 meters ● 15 March 1965

There is an arms race among marine organisms, though generally it seems to have some sanity to it. The lionfish is endowed with venom spines, but not overendowed, for its distinctive body markings, which advertise its dangerousness, might hinder the animal's ability to feed on other fishes. However, they are fairly abundant on the reef, so the advantages of venom glands coupled with poster markings must outweigh the disadvantages.

178. Peacock Lionfish *Pterois volitans* (Linnaeus) ● 3/4 life size ● Turtle Bay, Watamu, Kenya ● 4 meters ● 12 October 1966

Lionfishes are quite aware of their armament, for they are bold. Large fishes may have experimented with them, to their mutual discomfort, but it is obvious when one swims with lionfishes that they have little fear, or if they are afraid, they first display before retreating from a persistent diver.

Unlike the stonefishes, some lionfishes, particularly the Red Sea and Peacock lionfishes, are active during the day and swim openly around coral heads in search of a meal. One summer, in Belau, I was photographing a Peacock lionfish. As I observed the animal through my camera, the fish lowered his head, bringing the dorsal spines forward. He faced off with the camera and charged it, stopping short of collision. Two other lionfish were nearby, off to my side. Since my undiminutive presence could provoke an attack, real or feigned, I suddenly felt insecure when all three fish were not in full view.

179. Bandit Puffer *Arothron nigropunctatus* (Bloch & Schneider) ● Mountain Coral *Porites sp.* ● Soft Corals ● Life size ● The Creek, Red Sea, Obhor Kuraa, Saudi Arabia ● 12 meters ● 10 March 1965

While certain fishes and other marine animals are venomous, some, including the bandit puffer, are poisonous when eaten. Puffers puff up by gulping water, like their relatives, the bridled burrfish and porcupinefishes. Unlike them, they do not have protective spines. Their protection is their poisonous skin, liver, gonads, and intestines. The poison acts on the nerves. When a human is poisoned, symptoms develop within ten to forty-five minutes. The tongue and lips begin to tingle, a condition that may then spread to the entire body. Numbness follows, along with extreme weakness, nausea, excessive salivation, and stomach pains. As the body shuts down operations, muscles begin to twitch, and one's voice departs; swallowing becomes difficult, and finally there are convulsions, respiratory paralysis, and death.

In view of these gruesome facts, it is all the more surprising that the Japanese regard puffer meat as a delicacy. Some restaurants have specially trained fugu cooks to prepare the edible parts of the puffer, and the odds of surviving a professionally prepared meal are probably good.

In Belau the fishermen have a different way of eating puffer. They spear and eat only "the big puffer," which is not poisonous. "The little poisonous one" they leave alone.

180. Speckled Moray Eel *Gymnothorax sp.* ● Crustose Coralline Algae ● Life size ● Isla Daphne, Galápagos Islands, Ecuador ● 10 meters ● 23 March 1974

Less than man, more than human, king and jester, you charm me with your smile. I dived with you, and I discovered no evil anywhere. Shadows of darkness surround you, but you and they are as innocent as the water, the sky, and the sun.

INDEX

ACKNOWLEDGMENTS

*Throughout the preparation of this book there have been
several individuals who have given generously of their time,
understanding and expertise. Sally Faulkner is indebted to
Nicolas Ducrot, whose unfailing support has helped nurture and sustain the book;
to Harvey Horowitz for his guidance and oft-needed humor and warmth;
to Walter Eitel and Nina Kowaloff who patiently contributed their talents;
and to John Kings for his intelligent editing. Special appreciation is warmly extended to
Barry Fell for his enthusiastic willingness to be part of this book when it was still a concept.*

For their help over the years, out of which this book grew, we wish to thank:
Haruo Adelbai, Cesare Antoniacci, Chuichi Araga, James Atz, Edward Barnard,
Frederick Bayer, George Benjamin, Uldekel and Ermang Besebs, Tewid Boisek, Warren Burgess,
Ida Catala-Stucki, Drayton Cochran, Maureen Downey, William Emerson, Robert Endean,
Thomas Ermang, Louis Eschembrenner, Seymour and Alice Faulkner, Herbert Forgash,
Carl Gage, Charles and Julianne Golding, Ward and Maryke Griffioen, Ann Guilfoyle,
Willard Hartman, Patricia Hunt, Leon and Audrey Israel, Finn Jensen, Leonard Jossel,
Idesmang Kitalong, Singer Kochi, Ernest Lachner, Milton Liberty, Les Line,
Isadore Lipson, Heath and Judy McLendon, Yves and Germaine Merlet, David Miller,
Phyllis Montgomery, Elliott and Phyllis Nagelberg, Sylvain Napoleon,
William Old, Demei Otobed, Robert and Hera Owen, Toshiro Paulis, David Pawson,
John Randall, Richard Randall, Reg and Shirley Rice, Ronn Ronch,
Victor Springer, Takeshi Suzuki, Ted and Mae Tansy, Huzio Utinomi,
Richard Vahan, Anders Wästfelt, Peter and Ann Wilson, Robert Woodward.

Concept and design by Douglas Faulkner

Editorial coordination by Sally Faulkner

Special color work by Quality Color Laboratory,
New York, New York

Printed and bound by Roto Sadag, S.A.,
Geneva, Switzerland